HOME STAND

HOME STAND

GROWING UP IN SPORTS

• James McKean

Michigan State University Press • *East Lansing*

♾ The paper used in this publication meets the minimum requirements
of ANSI/NISO 39.48-1992 (R 1997) (Permanence of Paper).

Michigan State University Press
East Lansing, Michigan 48823-5245

Printed and bound in the United States of America.

11 10 09 08 07 06 05 1 2 3 4 5 6 7 8 9 10

LIBRARY OF CONGRESS CATALOGING-IN-PUBLICATION DATA
McKean, James, 1946 July 4–
Home stand : growing up in sports / James McKean.
p. cm.
ISBN 0-87013-749-2 (cloth : alk. paper)
1. McKean, James, 1946 July 4—Childhood and youth. 2. Authors, American—20th century—Biography. 3. Sports—Anecdotes. I. Title.
PS3563.C3737M34 2005
2004025890

Cover design by Heather Truelove Aiston
Book design/composition by Sharp Des!gns, Inc.
Cover photo is used courtesy of Washington State University

green press INITIATIVE Michigan State University Press is a member of the Green Press Initiative and is committed to developing and encouraging ecologically responsible publishing practices. For more information about the Green Press Initiative and the use of recycled paper in book publishing, please visit *www.greenpressinitiative.com*

Visit Michigan State University Press on the World Wide Web at *www.msupress.msu.edu*

• *for Penny and Meryl*

For a long important while I didn't have to think, except as an athlete does. I just played ball. Sweet moves and the ball in the hole. The pure poetry that satisfies when you're young.

—Stephen Dunn

CONTENTS

ACKNOWLEDGMENTS

GRATEFUL ACKNOWLEDGMENT IS MADE TO THE EDITORS OF THE following books and magazines in which versions of these chapters first appeared:

"Wallula Junction" in *Crab Orchard Review* (Fall/Winter 2000); "Recoveries" in *Father Nature: Fathers as Guides to the Natural World* (University of Iowa Press, 2003), edited by Paul Piper and Stan Tag; "One on One" and "Learning to Fight" in the *Gettysburg Review* (Summer 1998 and Summer 2004), reprinted here with the acknowledgment of the editors; "Split Bamboo" in *Gray's Sporting Journal* (May/June 2003); "D/Altered" in the *Iowa Review* (Spring 2004); "Fade-Away" in the *Nebraska Review* (Summer 2002); "Playing for Jud" in *Witness* (vol. 16, no. 1 [2002]).

"Playing for Jud" was reprinted in *Best American Sports Writing 2003* (Houghton Mifflin, 2003), edited by Buzz Bissinger and Glenn Stout.

The excerpt from Robert Creeley's "I Know a Man" is from his *Collected Poems of Robert Creeley, 1945–1975*, copyright © 1983 by the Regents of the University of California. Reprinted by permission of the University of California Press.

The excerpt from Robert Lowell's "Waking Early Sunday Morning" (*Near the Ocean*) is from *Collected Poems* by Robert Lowell. Copyright © 2003 by Harriet Lowell and Sheridan Lowell. Printed by permission of Farrar, Straus and Giroux, L.L.C.

My thanks to good friends and readers who gave time and attention to these essays: Mary Curran, Carol Deering, Paul Diehl, Bill Ford, Cecile Goding, Jim Grove, and Gordon Mennenga. Many thanks and much gratitude to Bob Grunst and Paul Zimmer, who have seen me through this book from start to finish. Their encouragement, good sense, critical insight, and friendship have sustained me for many years. Finally, thanks to my family and especially my wife, Penny, who is my best reader. They set the standard, sat in the stands, and cheered me on.

INTRODUCTION

NOT LONG AGO, RAY STEIN, A BASKETBALL TEAMMATE OF MINE AT Washington State University, sent me a videotape of a game we played against UCLA in Pullman on January 7, 1967. A gift of our mutual history, the tape itself was a copy of a sixteen-millimeter game film taken by the UCLA coaching staff. I have known the outcome of this game for thirty-five years, the box scores published and archived. Now, more evidence in hand, I tapped my finger against the plastic case to see if anything was still alive. Why did I feel so hesitant about watching?

Thirty-five years. Maybe I was afraid that what I remembered after all this time—and whatever heroics, if any, I credited myself with—stood in stark contrast to this long-sequestered witness. The young man in the film doesn't exist any more; or maybe he does, in a far slower and heavier version, only his conceptual hoops left. Maybe I needed to prepare myself first by acknowledging all those who had helped me, and the serendipity and luck I had growing up, so that I might play basketball at all, let alone against UCLA here on this tape.

How all the games reel back. At thirteen, sitting in the fall assembly at Morgan Junior High in Seattle, I was more than a little envious of Tommy Stackhouse, who walked up to the stage before the Morgan Junior High student body to receive his "Outstanding Seventh Grade Athlete" trophy. So far, the only recognition I'd had in eighth grade was from the vice-principal, who called me in to accuse me of flashing a hypodermic needle at a Morgan football game in which Tommy Stackhouse probably ran for a touchdown. Well, Mickey Scott, my neighbor, had found the hypo in his parents' attic—two glass vials with dull needles, and the metal plunger apparatus that opened on a hinge—and traded it to me for a model airplane, a B-17. My excuse to Mr. Reiss, the vice-principal, was that I was taking it to Mr. Benson, the science teacher, to place in his hands for "science," but forgot it in my backpack until the game. I wouldn't have needed the story if Mary Parkins had kept her mouth shut, but she told all her friends, and one of them told her mother, who called the school to say some weird kid was threatening to inject her daughter with Clorox.

Not true, I told my parents, who looked incredulous but said OK, as long as I boxed the hypo up and delivered it as explained in my narrative. It was a good story I had to stick with, though probably everybody saw through it and came to the conclusion I needed something constructive to occupy my time.

Then we moved to Tacoma. In the middle of eighth grade. I didn't want to be Mr. Science anymore, having been stuck for two weeks on the ratio for pulleys. I tried out for judo instead.

° ° °

WHEN I ASKED MY FATHER IF HE HAD MONEY FOR INSURANCE so that I could play football my sophomore year at Wilson High School in Tacoma, Washington, he dug through his wallet to see. I had good hands, and visions of long bombs and diving catches.

"Sorry," he said, and folded his wallet and stuck it back in his pocket. That's that. Naturally I had asked at the last minute, and the deadline for the football insurance payment and sign-up passed as I was trying to organize the rest of my fifteen-year-old life.

A week later, I asked if he had insurance money for my playing basketball, the sign-up deadline for that sport approaching soon.

"How much?" he asked.

"Six bucks," I said. "I can pay you back in a couple of weeks."

"No. That's OK," he said, pulling out his wallet and handing me a five and a one. "Just make sure you sign up."

I would like to thank my father here for that little deception, although at fifteen I didn't recognize what he was trying to do. He knew football. He knew football players, his brother-in-law being a star lineman in the thirties for the University of Washington. My father had the money, I'm sure now, as well as the vision of me, his incredibly skinny son, outstretched for the long bomb the instant before my dismemberment. "Play basketball," his six bucks told me. And I did.

I would like to thank Jack Johnson, my junior high school basketball coach who cut me in the eighth grade, probably because judo taught me only how to fall down, and finally let me start when I was in the ninth. After that, I lost touch with him until I was playing for Washington State. One evening, Jack walked onto the court as one of our Pac-8 referees. Before five thousand people and the opposing benches, at the height and tension and volume of the game, Jack Johnson handed me the ball at the free throw line and said, "Remember what I taught you in the ninth grade."

"That I never get called for fouls?"

"You wish," he laughed, and proceeded to talk at me for the rest of the game. In the sixties, I remember how the good officials in the Pac-8 (Ernie Filiberti and Mel Ross, for example) held conversations with the players during the games—coded and brief, certainly; short, clipped instructions; a warning here and there; even a compliment or two. And if you listened and nodded or even asked a question, you understood their limits and consequently yours: "Watch the hands. Give ground or I'll call that next time. Good move. Good shot. That was clean. Good 'D.'"

Only Jack Johnson added, "I taught you everything you know."

If teaching is opportunity and attention, then yes, he set my odd basketball career in motion. He let me play—tall, gangly, slow-footed, but sure-handed and a good shot—and undoubtedly passed the word to the Wilson High School coaches that a prospect, albeit raw, was on his way up.

I would like to thank them, too—Dan Inveen, Joe Stortini, John Sinkovich—wise men they appeared to me, old, approaching thirty maybe. But I was fifteen, shy, myopic, and growing. Nothing seemed to fit, neither clothes nor social scenes nor the maniacal hallways through which I wandered to class. I hadn't attended Wilson High School two weeks when Inveen, the head basketball coach, stopped me in the hallway and said that he was glad that I had signed up for basketball, and asked if he could he see my schedule.

"No, no, this won't do," he said. "Come on. We'll get it fixed." I waited outside the counselor's office, and when Inveen came back out, he handed me a revised class schedule with the last three periods of the day now reading Study Hall, Gym, and Free Period. "Study Hall will be in the gym. Suit up and get some work done."

For those two months before basketball practice started, each of the next three years, I had the gym more or less to myself. I'd shoot and shoot. Every so often, one of my coaches or teachers, these old men all of thirty, would show up to play one-on-one. We'd talk some about the game, study a variety of moves, and then play, hard, winner keeps the ball. Always surprised how fast they were and how strong and how little compassion they had for pain, I'd try to fend them off or shoot over the top or move faster and faster until the bell rang and they had somewhere to get to. I stayed in the gym. Shift two had already showed up, shooting at a corner basket, waiting to play one-on-one.

It saved me. Kept me focused. By the time my senior season was over, all that time in the gym had earned me a basketball scholarship to Washington State University three hundred miles across the state in Pullman. What I left behind were good basketball stats, a picture of me in uniform in the Wilson High School trophy case, and an institutional set of expectations for my brother, who is five-and-a-half years younger than me. The moment he set foot on Wilson High's grounds, he started hating me. The better I played at Washington State—my father collecting clippings, and my brother's teachers (Coach Inveen included) saying congratulations to him for my success and mentioning all season the size of my shoes—the more my brother avoided that trophy case, then the hallway itself, and finally the very mention of my name.

"That picture isn't really me, you know," I told my brother years later over beer. "It's more a celebration of the uniform." This issue has long been settled in both our lives after athletics—mine to teaching and poetry, and his to the Coast Guard, tugboats in Alaska, and then the shipyards in Bremerton, Washington. Now we address concerns about our aging mother and tell stories about the years we hardly knew each other, about growing up in a family that loved sports, about our father, who would rather go salmon fishing than do almost anything else, and about our uncle and aunt, the football player and the Olympic swimmer, who hounded their children and nieces and nephews with the intensity of coaches, which is what they were.

That picture of me in the uniform doesn't do justice to those times, I try to explain to my brother, thinking of the complications of the sixties and seventies. "Yeah, tell me about it," he says. "And you weren't even home."

I would like to thank my daughter for letting me down gently. I encouraged her to play basketball, of course, and she did in school. From the stands, I thought I saw something of myself in the way she moved, a little too upright, shuffling spot to spot, then quick to the ball and quick to release, good hands and a good touch.

But oh, how the game, the competition itself, frustrated her. Given a choice, she would rather read a book. After sitting on the bench game after game because of a twisted ankle, she said one day, "You know, Dad, how parents sometimes, especially parents who were athletes themselves, pressure their kids into sports because the parents want to relive their own childhood?"

"I haven't got a clue what you're getting at," I said, but she knew I was lying. I knew that basketball for her would be just another school activity like flute or the science fair. That she would abandon the game and its simple narrative, and then worry that I might be disappointed.

Yes and no. That's OK. She would rather hear the stories, curious about her own prehistory, where and whom she is from. She's willing to keep me company as we watch the videotape—artifact of my life, and in some ways hers too—silent, in black and white. The original film has been edited and clipped. It's as if we're sitting in the back row, looking between the fans standing up in front of us, the game about to begin with a jump ball between Lew Alcindor and a thin young man with a full head of hair. "There I am," I say, touching the screen, "number 42."

We watch in silence the silent game. I think of my aunt watching herself swim in a film of the 1936 Olympics, and realize how much she still remembered and what she still felt about that event, and where it stood in her life at the time—the film simply a prompt, one of many shards she reassembled in memory. I squint at the screen to see if I can tell what I was feeling or thinking, but the film lacks focus and we're too far away. I know the outcome. My daughter groans in sympathy as Lew Alcindor backs in, turns, and scores easily, one of his eleven baskets. But I'm not counting. Instead, I see a Washington State player at the high post when the low post is his natural position; a player who passes well (I had forgotten that or merely discounted it); a player who stands too upright but moves quickly enough, and has open shots but hurries them; a player who tries too hard and loses just enough touch, consequently, to miss; who works hard enough to make a few shots and grab a few rebounds, but still seems a step slow and two feet too short and tired by the end.

We lose this game, but not by much. At the time, UCLA was ranked number one in the country, and they beat us that night by nine points—UCLA's slimmest margin of victory so far that season.

"You remind me of me," my daughter says, the tape rewinding. And I'm pleased. I remember watching her from the stands and telling myself to keep quiet. "A little slow up and down the floor, but quick to the ball," she says. I explain to her how disappointed I am at my own play, surprised at how analytical and critical I am of number 42's performance, as if I could make him better.

"But it's just a tape," she says. "Nothing's going to change."

She's right. All reruns will be the same, the outcome on the scoreboard given to the last sixteen-millimeter frame, and then the screen goes blank, the stats boxed up, the win and loss recorded, the players in a newspaper photo suspended permanently in midair. Such is the static nature of facts. Such is the outside view, high in the stands, peering around heads at a game a long way off.

But sitting here, I remember from inside that game, looking up into the ambiguous stands and then down at the ref, who holds the ball up ready for the center jump. And just like that, the game begins again. And then others. How we got there comes back, and where we went afterward, and how each game distilled into simplicity a complex and dynamic time. As if no years had passed, my father explains how to troll for salmon, how to concentrate and read the water, how to hit a baseball or lift a ball to the basket. Then all my coaches are fretting again. The smell of each gym lies in my clothes. Lockers shut and locked, our teams walk single file and quiet back up the stairs, through the crowded doors, and onto the floor, both teams warming up. Lights and noise, the band starts up, Converse shoes screeching on a hundred different floors, and then the buzzer calls.

HOME STAND

RECOVERIES

I NEVER TOLD MY FATHER THIS, BUT LATE ONE NIGHT, HOME FROM college, I nearly lost his car on the street in front of the house he and my mother lived in, in Tacoma.

Beneath the front-porch light (it was too late even for moths), I pushed the key into the lock pin by pin to disturb no one, wobbly from beer and the cool, dark morning hours; but prodded by something, maybe the fear of being seen, I looked back over my shoulder. As if trying to sneak away, my father's robin's-egg blue '62 Ford station wagon was rolling backward down Huson Drive and gaining speed.

In the sobriety of adrenalin, I caught the car twelve strides later. The tires chirped when I hit the brakes, but there was no other sound that late night—no lights on suddenly, no last cricket to accompany my heart thudding for the imagined crunch of fenders and quarter panels, and the tinkle of glass. I started the car again, reparked it, held the shift in park, and set the parking brake. Hadn't I done that?

My father may have been watching, but never said. He was always watching, but sometimes could only shake his head at what he saw. At the fate of each of his new cars, for example. As if clean lines and new paint blinded her, my mother scraped their new '52 Mercury against a light standard. His new '55 Ford sedan my mother backed into the neighbor's car. His new '61 Ford station wagon I backed into a telephone pole late one night, three days after I had earned my driver's license. He was asleep when I got home, and I tossed and turned in bed, worrying about what I was going to say to him. The next morning, the heel of my right hand was scraped raw, and I remembered a nightmare wrapping me in tentacles. But I didn't remember trying to pound my way through the bedroom door that opened inward, yelling, until my father finally shoved the door open, grabbed me by the shoulders, and shook. "OK," I said. "I'm home."

° ° °

My mother was worried, she said on the phone. "Your father sits in the car in the driveway and won't come in." I was attending Washington State University at the time, three hundred miles across the state. I thought of my father's solitary side—the rock wall he built by himself in their backyard with a shovel and crowbar, for example. In the summer I would find him, late afternoons, resetting stones and whispering to no one. He wore black work pants and a T-shirt and a baseball hat, and would stop to talk a moment.

"Can I help?" I'd ask. He'd say thanks, but no, and I would climb back past all the asters and hydrangeas my mother had planted in the small plot of ground he worked for years to shore up.

It's as if he took it on himself to frame our lives, and within those frames permit the spontaneous and wild. When I think back, he always left something undone in his own life, something a little wild. When I was very young, we lived at the north end of Seattle in a small house on 171st Street. My father's first landscaping project was to build a river-rock wall around the front yard's madrone tree. But the madrone would not be contained.

I will never forget the litter of that tree—bark peeling, the leaves falling, a fecundity of trash that I was asked to rake up twice a week. The tree knew no seasons, no moderation, and dropped dinner-plate-size, indestructible pitch-coated leaves all over my father's new front lawn. Their disposal was my job, along with the strips of bark and the tree's waxy red berries. It was worse than dishes or laundry. I hated the front yard.

However, the backyard had potential. Although my father built a cedar fence six feet high and planted his lawn and flower beds, he left one corner, maybe a quarter of the yard, unfinished. There he dumped peat moss and, one horrible summer, a pile of manure for my mother's flower gardens. The rest of the ground I laid claim to. I dug traps, more intrigued by the deadfall and the camouflage than by what I might catch. I started fires, set up tents, built a lean-to, dug in a home plate from which I drove baseballs that loosened the nails of his fence. He let me do all this. He even set up a regulation ten-foot basket that I couldn't reach for years.

The fence marked the limit. At first I couldn't climb over it, but the taller I grew, the easier it was to vault. Into Mr. Ruland's yard, past the neighbor's dog—gone spastic with barking—and into the woods. My father had no intention, I believe, of enclosing anybody, but he wanted me to know that there were benevolent limits where he made his presence known—where he stood, in effect.

After I could finally get the ball up to the rim, my father stood on the sidelines for years, watching me play basketball. When I played at Wilson High School, I remember asking him each morning for a ride home after practice, which ended each evening at 5:30. Invariably he was there at 5:00, and sometimes 4:30, standing in the doorway to watch. He attended all the games, though he said little afterwards besides "Good game," or nothing, in sympathy, if we lost. Once, in a game against Bremerton (the Black Knights, who played dirty—the Navy kids from the other side of the Sound), I grew tired of the pinching and the fist in the kidneys and the rooting out on rebounds, and threw an elbow that caught my opponent in the temple. It was a sucker punch I'd planned since halftime, and before the Black Knight stood back up, I had run down the court. After the game, which we won, my father seemed more silent than usual. Full of myself for the victory and for my assault, I asked if he had seen my well-placed elbow.

"I wish I hadn't," he replied, and then drove on in silence. It was what such mean behavior deserved—the threat of his absence. Devastated by that, I knew immediately how petty that elbow was, and worse, how inappropriate my crowing about it. The chill rode home with us.

All those years I was growing up, his teaching was an articulation of place—Sekiu and Neah Bay on the Strait of Juan de Fuca, Point No Point and Hat Island on Puget Sound, the Hoh River, La Push and the Quillayute River, Westport and Ilwaco on the Pacific Ocean. He wanted to fish, and he took me along. From Seattle, we would drive south through Olympia and then up through Humptulips and Queets into the Olympic Peninsula, the two-lane road a tunnel through trees where logging trucks roared. I remember once, outside Forks, a load of cut and cleaned cedar logs, three feet in diameter at the butt ends, lay topsy-turvy beside the road. "Busted loose," my father said, and for miles I imagined every logging truck on every curve tipping as we passed, air brakes growling, the chains snapping, and twenty tons of cedar logs rolling our car flat like pie dough.

"Look, look," he would say, and there would be deer or elk in a field. One time, in the narrow road of the rain forest, a cougar on the center stripe looked hard at us before it leapt into the green.

Sometimes we took a ferry across Puget Sound and Hood Canal, and drove north through Sequim and Port Angeles, and up the road past the one tavern and gas pump of Pysht, Washington—"Psst," he'd say every time, and then, "Too late, you missed it"—and finally, late into Sekiu, where we parked next to Olson's boathouse, peed in the woods behind, and found bedsprings leaning against the wall and an old smelly mattress to sleep on. In the corner behind kicker boats overturned and stacked, we would lay the mattress out and sweep it with the flashlight beam and brush away the mouse turds and unroll our sleeping bags. Lying there trying to sleep next to my father, I could smell the salt air and boathouse oil, and listen to the fog horn and sometimes the clack and rumble of a late logging train rolling down from the forest into Sekiu to dump its logs into the Strait.

For a boy, it was all wonderful—the scrambled eggs, pancakes, and orange juice the next morning at the Cove Café, the bait shop with its Day-Glo panorama of lures, chrome flashers, and buckets of lead. From the trunk of our car, my father hauled his fifteen-horse Evinrude down to our rented sixteen-foot kicker boat tied at the dock; then the gas can, frozen herring, a cooler of sandwiches, rain gear, life jackets, poles and tackle box, net, and compass for the front seat. Early we would push out into the Strait, everything we needed stowed in our boat. Beyond its gunwales, beneath the great green rollers, hid the salmon we had come so far for. My line disappeared into the swells. And up rose seals and box jellyfish and kelp and schools of pilot whales, and once the black-and-white back of an orca rolling up not ten feet from our boat, the dorsal fin taller than me. There were gulls and ling cod and halibut, and every once in a while the *tap tap* at the line, and then the pull and set, the winding, and a coho would work its way up until silver flashed in green water thirty feet from the boat, and out it would leap like a trout, head shaking.

My father loved the self-contained rhythms of fishing, the ritual of an early start, the catch and the tending to it, and maybe most of all, the solitude. Once in La Push, he took me to the commercial boat docks in the evening when the long liners motored up beside the dock to weigh their catch, fish by fish, in the broker's scale. Many of these one-man trollers didn't seem much bigger than our kicker boat, with a small cabin and outriggers above hand winches, and two-cylinder inboard diesels wheezing thump by thump at idle. My father said they'd store up on ice and stay out several days, and when they caught enough they'd come in over the bar and wait in line here.

The one fisherman I remember, bearded, in oil slickers, reached into his hold to lay silver salmon after salmon at the feet of the broker, who weighed two or three at a time in the scales, bright fish five to eight pounds apiece. And when the fisherman stood straight up a moment as if to rest his back, the broker opened his book to write a check on the spot. "One more," that fisherman said, in the best of dramatic pauses, and reached down into the ice and lifted with effort a huge king onto the dock. It made up ten of those silvers, maybe fifty or sixty pounds, and deserved a scale all to itself. Strangers glanced at each other and took a breath, and the broker crumpled his first check and commenced to write another. I could see on my father's face that a small, self-contained fishing boat on the Pacific Ocean would suit him just fine. He told me years later, when he was about to retire, that he wanted to buy an Airstream and park it overlooking the Pacific at Westport. He thought he could get a job as a bait boy, anything to keep on the water. As it turned out, my mother had other plans.

° ° °

"SHOOT THEM ALL OFF BEFORE WE GO HOME," MY FATHER warned. I was born on the Fourth of July, and at thirteen wasn't more than a short hormonal fuse away from exploding myself. That Fourth of July weekend, as our family was driving to Mukilteo, Washington, I was surprised when he stopped at a fireworks stand and said, "Pick out something." Of course, I chose the six-dollar Racket Box. Not one pretty thing on the contents list. It had Black Cats and Thunder Bombs and M-88s and Lady Fingers and Yankee Boys, and every assortment of noise from buzz to bang.

We were on our way to Hat Island—six nautical miles off Mukilteo and three miles around—and for one weekend and the island's entire circumference, I held small wars with sea gulls, dented cans, blew up bunkers and driftwood houses, launched sand crabs, exploded kelp bulbs and stubborn clams, and lifted up geysers of water with cherry bombs. I stirred the outhouses, singed my fingernails, blew my hair back, and never in three days risked an aesthetic moment. The last act of my noise symphony was the mortar (maybe an eighth of a stick of TNT) to be shot straight up from its stand, the final salute. When I lit it and backed away that early evening, however, the wind blew it over, and down the boardwalk and under the cabin's porch my bomb skipped. Oh, how my mother and father and their friends, John and Helen, jumped, the flash and roar two feet beneath their wicker chairs. "Bravo, bravo," I thought I heard someone say, but my hearing hadn't been right all weekend.

It was not the last time I would complicate the best-laid plans, mine or my father's. When I was courting Penny, now my wife, my father asked us if we would like to go charter-fishing at Westport, one of my father's favorite activities. The ritual was as follows: 3:30 A.M. departure from Tacoma, a stop at the Aberdeen café for breakfast and fish talk—always the weather, and either old stories retold or speculation about the day's possibilities, tides, and catch patterns. A license at the bait shop, the sky near blue. Then, gathering on the dock before the charter boat—this time a small six-person boat—the dawn departure, crossing the bar at the mouth of Gray's Harbor, a dramatic ride on the incoming rollers, and then a ride out the buoy line.

I could see that despite her preparation with Dramamine, Penny looked pale and queasy down in the hold. "Don't stay in the cabin," I advised, trying to sound authoritative. After all, I had never been seasick in all the times fishing with my father on the Sound or out here on the Pacific, and I took this as a point of pride.

When we finally motored far enough out, the captain cut the engine and we placed ourselves around the boat, my father at his favorite spot in the bow. I showed Penny how to rig her line, explaining how the cut-plug herring impaled on two hooks spins to mimic a live fish, how many strips of line to let out, and what to do if a fish took the bait. I knew everything, stood beside her as resident authority, having done this with my father for years. Such is the odd mix of love and hubris, a kind of lure, of course, for cosmic irony.

For it allowed me to hook the first fish on the boat, even before I could light the cigarette I held in my lips. There was the strike, the *tap tap,* and I set the hooks. I felt blessed. A salmon running. "Fish on, fish on," I yelled, and moved sideways along the rail as the fish ran out at an angle away from the boat. Line zipped out, my Penn reel spraying water. The rod *jerk-jerk*ed and then lightened up, and I reeled as fast as I could because the fish was running back toward the boat. *No slack,* I heard my father say in the back of my mind. *Rod tip up.* And then the fish turned again, and I crab-walked against the rail toward the stern of the boat that reared up at that moment on a wave. As the salmon tore straight out, I leaned forward against the brass chain that guarded the only open spot in the boat railing, the two-foot-wide entrance we had stepped though onto the boat an hour before, the chain that held my kneecaps and my bravado, the chain I trusted.

Balance never seems precarious until you lose it. Then it's gone. Simple and certain. No decision, no analysis, no argument, not a single negotiation would have changed my falling headfirst in a great and slow-motion arc into the sea. My glasses unhinged from my face and tumbled away, but no matter. I was not going to lose my father's sacred fishing rod, and witnesses on the boat, befuddled for a moment by my amazing disappearance, testified they saw first a tip-top guide, then a rod rising out of the sea, a reel, my hand, and then my head popping up beside the boat. The first thing I saw was Penny looking down, no longer pale. "What should I do?" she asked.

"Take the rod, please," I said. "Take the rod."

Next to her, my father said, "Oh, Christ, what now?" and shaking his head, leaned down and grabbed my belt with one hand and my coat collar with the other. He was a big man, over six-foot-three inches tall and weighing 250, and though I am big enough in my own right and was waterlogged at that moment, it didn't seem to matter. My father winched me out of the sea and dropped his biggest catch of the day, dripping and puffing, onto the deck. It happened so fast the shirt beneath my coat stayed dry. I still had the filter of my cigarette, the tobacco and paper washed away, clamped in my lips. I looked around. The captain of our charter boat blabbed into his CB radio the news that would make me famous in Westport. Penny handed me the rod, and I lifted and wound the reel and found, to my surprise, the fish still hooked.

Years later, I wrote a poem in which that fish escaped. I took Richard Hugo's advice and changed the triggering story so that "my salmon / [with] one last desperate leap / shakes the hook free." I'm glad I did. The historical truth, however, is that I caught the fish, and the next night back in Tacoma, my father barbecued salmon fillets, and my mother made potato salad and tartar sauce, and we drank toasts to good fishing and even better recoveries. By the next day the story was taking on a life of its own, and would develop over a decade of salmon dinners as mildly heroic or sometimes cautionary, but always comic. My father admired that I had still caught the fish. Penny said she was afraid I might drown and forgot all about her seasickness. "Weren't you worried?" she asked my father.

"He can swim," he said, without a fuss.

I was especially glad I hadn't lost his fishing gear, although I squinted hard until my next pair of glasses. Given her experience at sea, I was elated that Penny accepted my proposal of marriage. When we told my father over dinner one night, he toasted us and wrote the date and our names on the wine cork. It felt like a handing over, and the fact that corks float escaped none of us. By this time, my father fished less and less, and spent more and more time trimming his yard and edging and turning stone after stone before his never-finished rock wall. Flowers bloomed all around his house, and the fir trees in his backyard grew so tall they blocked his view of Mount Rainier. Shadows fell for him earlier each day. Out of sight down by the back fence, he still had his horseshoe pits where he and Mr. Nordheim, his eighty-five-year-old neighbor, competed. Clear up at the house, you could hear the ringing, and Mr. Nordheim swearing in Norwegian.

At the end of his life, I'm sure my father thought I could fall out of most any boat and get back in, though I felt he stood close by and watched. I still feel that way. It's a comfort and a measure. After Penny and I were married, he gave me a scrapbook he had tended season by basketball season—my basketball records, team pictures, basketball articles from the *Tacoma News Tribune* and the *Spokesman-*

Review, programs of the games he had attended, stat sheets—a whole history of my basketball career. He had collected it all by himself, as simply and as thoughtfully as he shored up my mother's gardens. This was the first I knew of it.

∘ ∘ ∘

MY MOTHER MUST HAVE ASKED HIM FINALLY WHAT HE WAS DOING sitting out in the car after dark with the neighbors watching. "Listening to Jim's game on the radio," he told her. When Washington State played in Oregon or Idaho, or simply at home in Pullman, three hundred miles away, my father would sit in his driveway and search the car's radio for the game. It was the 1960s. AM radio was the band of choice, and when the ionosphere lifted after dusk, signals skipped in from a long way off. He would drive until he found the game and the best reception, and then park, invariably in front of his own house on that hill in Tacoma. Through the static and distance, he found me and listened by himself.

When I think of my father, I try to listen carefully. Throughout my growing up, "Think, think," he would say, my ten-penny nails bent, a fender dented, another hasty choice based on too few facts. I'd listen hard to my thoughts fading in and out. "Slow down," he would say. This from a man, like many, who had worked his way through poverty and war. What I know is that he was deliberate and thoughtful and always there for me in his solitude—and then he was gone. As often as I can, I string a rod and stand in a river. Or rent a boat to drift across a calm lake and fish until dusk. Or sometimes I simply drive late at night and listen to the radio. The reception is far better then for distant places and time.

SPLIT BAMBOO

TURNED JUST SO, SALMON SCALES DRIED ON BAMBOO GLINT LIKE morning sun off the Sound. In memory, a clinker boat pushes off, clear of the shore and drifting. After my father died, my mother gave me his bamboo rod and old Penn reel, fishing gear I had heard about many times but never seen, my father having opted long ago for lighter and shorter fiberglass salmon rods. For some reason he had not cleaned the bamboo rod, and after years of attics and basements, it had fallen into disrepair, the varnish water-damaged and peeling, the guide wraps rotten, the ferrule loose. When I tried to insert the tip into the butt piece, the ferrule slipped, but the two halves held together enough so I could hold the rod out and imagine trolling for salmon. When I lightly scraped each bamboo section, the scales fell clear, and I could see where my father, just above the handle, had written his name.

All the pieces were there. I notched the huge Penn reel into the rod seat, screwed the down-locking ring, and held the outfit up to look at the reel's Bakelite handle and the diorama engraved in the plastic side beneath the clicker button—a small boat cresting a wave, rods in their holders pointing out the back and sides, a scene that could well be set in the strait off Sekiu, Washington, where my father loved to fish. A kicker boat rented from Olson's, so his story went—told at the dinner table or over beer every time my uncle visited from Portland—the climax always the fifty-two-pound king salmon my father caught on this bamboo rod.

I loved the language of his story. The gray day and the tide flowing. Cut-plugs and flashers. Silk leaders. Trolling off the slide and then over the hole, and then the bump and strike and the reel singing. By this time, my father had broken out from a secret place the kippered salmon, canned by my mother in Mason jars. The smell of smoked salmon and oil and sugar drifted through the kitchen. My mother sliced cheddar cheese and set another round of beer on the table, and I could tell, by the look on my uncle's face, that he was glad he had driven those five hours north on 99.

Oh, how a king sounds. Even very young, I understood the word two ways: the fish heading straight down, and the zinging of line from the reel—the Evinrude at idle, its exhaust growling as roller after roller lifted the boat. "Like hauling up plywood," my father would say. "No coho this time." A king for sure, a Chinook, a lunker, a Tyee, the great Northwest leviathan itself, coming up after an hour of aching arms, inch after inch, run after run, drop and wind and lift, until at last from the depth and all that wonder the dark-green back and silver sides boiled to the surface. "Boiled," my father would say again, and each time he told his story, my heart would gallop at the thought of it, his fish roiling in the waves, black eyes and hooked jaw and silver sides, my father and his friend John banging their knees trying to lead its head into the too-small net, the boat tipping, and finally, with the broad, flat tail dotted with sea lice the size of dimes sticking out the end of the net, they hoisted the king over the gunwale and set it, tail still flapping, in the bottom of the boat.

This was the very rod. The stories were part of fishing. In the requisite picture, my father in overalls and baseball hat stands outside a cabin in Sekiu and holds up his cleaned fifty-two-pound salmon and grins. In the foreground I stand oblivious, three years old, charmed by my own shoes. The fish weighs more than I do. Fifty years later, his split-bamboo rod was still flexible, but when I gave it a shake, two guides fell off and the ferrule dislodged completely. That's when I decided to get the rod refinished.

For several years I have attended the Hawkeye Fly Fishing Association's annual convention in some town in Iowa. My wife and I live in Iowa, and these gatherings seem a long way from Sekiu. Whether in Davenport or Waterloo or Altoona, each year Don Schroeder displays his handmade split-bamboo rods. Twelve hundred dollars apiece to start, they are beautiful trout rods, three weight to six weight, from five-and-a-half feet to eight feet long, two piece and three piece. I can't afford them, but stop at his table every year and admire the work and wonder why Don is so cranky. Some say this goes with the rod-building territory. When I finally summoned the courage to take my father's rod in to Don, I also found out he was deaf. I tried to tell him how important the rod was, how it had landed a fifty-two-pound salmon, but he was already pulling the rod from its ancient aluminum tube and flannel sock and squinting at the wraps and handle.

"Wrong ferrule," he said without looking at me. "Backwards. I've got the right one at home. Old South Bend Muskie rod." He turned the rod and looked it over and held it carefully, a jeweler's loupe the only thing missing from his examination.

"Could you fix it for me?" But he didn't look up until I pointed to my father's name and spoke up: "Could you save the name just like this if you refinish the rod?"

"Yes," he said, "but I'm busy. Too many shows. Leave it with me.

Maybe six months." He took my loose guides and slipped the rod halves back into their sock and then into the aluminum tube and set it behind him in a large stack of rod tubes. I began to worry. He wrote out a receipt and handed it to me: Total cost $100, half down now, please.

"This can't be right," I said, but he couldn't hear me. I wanted reassurance. What could $100 buy? How would he do this? But Don had turned abruptly away to other customers, perhaps turning both kinds of deaf ear, as I left my phone number and address and a check for the down payment.

Standing there empty-handed, I was left with nothing but a story that needed refinishing. It too was in pieces. Not so many years after that picture of my father had been taken, I wanted to catch a salmon just as he had so many times. I believe he worked hard to create the circumstances so that I might do just that. However, those circumstances were uncomfortable and required behaviors uncommon for the self-indulgent appetites of a ten-year-old.

Getting up at 5:00 A.M., for example. Those mornings on Hat Island, a small, steep-banked island in Puget Sound between Everett and Whidbey Island, the shadows were long and surreal. The cold was no dream, however, when my father shook me, saying it was time, come on now. Despite all my hesitation, I unzipped the warm sleeping bag, and the cold creosote smell in the back room of John's cabin flooded in. Jeans, my T-shirt and flannel shirt, coat and Little League baseball hat, and rubber boots. No fire yet in the stove. John and my father sat at the window, a thermos of coffee and sweet rolls in front of them, awaiting the first simple light.

The bay was silent and silver. No waves, and even if there had been we couldn't have heard them, for the tide was out a long way. The smell of the exposed seaweed and kelp and a kingdom of miniature crabs warmed to the morning and our boots as we pushed

John's boat back to the water. The keel scraped through the sand and round stones, the tide having left his clinker boat high and dry. The only commercial boat at Hat Island, a single-handed gillnetter moored in the bay, lay on its side next to its mooring buoy, which also lay on the sand next to its concrete anchor. Crisp salt air leaked under my collar.

We carried rods and gear and sandwiches assembled the night before. Seated in the bow, half asleep and huddled beneath my collar as John rowed deeper and deeper into the bay, I tried to remember the preparations from the night before, thinking if I could get them just right, then a salmon would surely strike my line. Late beneath the hissing kerosene lantern above the knotty-pine benches, John and my father talked about blackmouth and humpy runs. There were tide tables and speculations and seasons to discuss. A waxing (or was it a waning?) moon meant fewer fish the next morning, but larger and deeper, of course, and we would need four ounces of lead to fish the hole fifteen minutes out from the island's eastern point with its fish-robbing seals. As John and my father talked, they tied leaders to 2/0 Eagle Claw hooks, using a secret knot with wraps that looked like a hangman's knot around the hook's shaft just below the eye. Two hooks to a leader, one sliding above the other. Then they whetted the hooks, spit or oil the lubricant on a grooved stone, until the points scored their fingernails. Then they stretched the leaders straight, wound them back around their hands, slipped them off and into a leader wallet—its clear plastic sleeves like pages in a book—and leader after leader lay coiled in its speculations and strategies and story potential.

That morning John rowed farther out than usual, the Evinrude tilted up. The cabins grew smaller. When he pulled the oars in, I could see myself in the glass water. Then my face twirled and glinted below one eye and I disappeared altogether in a swirl. The water bubbled as if rain were falling up from the bottom. Standing now, my father lifted a long, thin piece of wood, picket-fence size but much longer, with nails driven into one edge and cut off and sharpened like teeth. He raked that wood down through the disturbed water as if paddling a canoe, and then pulled out of the Sound and held before us a row of brilliant, impaled fish. A herring rake, my father called it—a tool as ancient as the Nootka or Salish people, I read later. John and I plucked the herring off and into a bucket, and my father raked the water again. Soon we had enough bait for the morning, four- to six-inch herring swimming and ready. John released the Evinrude to upright, gave the primer bulb a squeeze, and pulled hard on the starter rope.

Waiting proved most difficult for me. After we had cleared the point, John cut the Evinrude and set the Mukilteo boat adrift, the wind pushing one way, the current another, so that the cut-plug herring worked its slow circular enticement forty strips down. Near the bow with my father, I felt the waves in my hands, the wind sometimes in the line hum, the occasional chucking of the boat, the rise and fall of rollers. Hunched sleepy in my coat and baseball hat, I wished for something to happen, sure this long, fishless wait was at best a penance, or at worst a deliberate cosmic snub. Each barren hour made me feel less worthy. Each toss of a wave pulled the line, but nothing happened no matter how I misread those slow and orderly rhythms. I'd imagine the *tap tap* and the sudden adrenaline pull. I'd count until a big roller lifted us, the seventh always, and the line pulled deeper. Then I'd count again.

We seemed to float above the Sound. Seagulls kept an eye on us. Suspended between the sea and the sky, I felt caught between being a child and those two men. I studied the shore—Whidbey Island, its beach houses, the lodgepole pines against the sky like torn paper, a wash of dark green and gray. I listened to the wind and recited names: "Point No Point, Deception Pass, Mukilteo." I had read the charts and memorized the depths and the shoals. I had collected lures and pieces of glass and driftwood and stones ground by the waves as if these things might serve as amulets. No matter. On that bow seat in the boat where John and my father put me, my impatience rose and fell, the horizon the only thing certain and stable, but a long way off.

I waited. I remember one time John set a new dime on the seat in front of me, a Roosevelt dime, and said it was mine when I caught my first fish. That made me even more impatient. Authentic, ringing silver, the dime shone like a small sun and never moved, though the boat rolled in the Sound. When I looked over the edge into the water, the sun hid behind my head, and rays extended out as if I were wearing a crown. If I caught a salmon, I thought, the sun would burn in my pocket.

In one of Hemingway's early dispatches to the *Toronto Star Weekly,* he wrote about tuna fishing in Vigo, Spain, explaining the sheer physical labor and hours of strain needed to land a three-hundred-pound Blue Fin tuna. When you finally "bring him up alongside the boat, green-blue and silver in the lazy ocean, you will be purified and be able to enter unabashed into the presence of the very elder gods and they will make you welcome." What I wanted at ten was to enter unabashed into the presence of my father and John Carlson, my father's most ardent fishing buddy. What they wanted was for me to learn how to fish and how to care for the world around me. I don't know if this is what they would have said, but it's what they did. They created opportunity after opportunity for me to do the same thing. Tenders and scavengers and husbands, these men worked all week to fish on the weekends, at Hat Island in Puget Sound, or Sekiu or Neah Bay on the Strait of Juan de Fuca, or sometimes during the summer all the way to La Push on the Pacific Ocean.

I doubt my father would have said that catching his fifty-two-pound king "purified" him. More likely he would have said that it "obliged" him to do something about it. Maybe it has to do with manners. I can hear his mother, my grandmother, saying, "Eat enough of what you are given, but everything you take." And we would. John and my father caught two small salmon off Hat Island that morning, and we brought them back to shore by way of the buoy and the crab traps. From the buoy—afloat again by the time we got back—hung a burlap sack full of butter clams I had dug the day before. John drifted the boat up close and we hauled in the gunnysack, the clams having spit out sand all night. Then he put the Evinrude in gear again and we motored across the bay in search of the crab traps, marked by wooden floats so small and green you almost had to know where they were to find them. The size of a steamer trunk and truly malevolent, with rebar frames and fishnet sides, the traps presented narrowing entrances at either end leading to fish guts and heads suspended at the center. Crabs could get in but not out. My father hauled the trap up by a rope that roared against the gunwale, and then tilted the trap into the boat, dripping and nightmarish with its claws and clacking and offal.

On shore, I was asked to identify the males and was shown how to hold them from the back to avoid the pinching claws. My father pried them apart and washed the pieces back and forth in the Sound. Then I watched him clean the salmon with a thin-bladed knife, also whetted the night before. He cut the gills, top and bottom, and pulled them out, bright red. Then he dipped his hand into the water and stroked the fish head to tail, turning it over and opening it with his knife from anal orifice to just below its chin.

At first my stomach backed up—an honest response, I think, to blood and the mysteries of internal organs—but my father went about it like he was opening a book. He took a moment to read the contents—orange roe or the yellow-white testes, young or old, out to or in from the sea, the stomach empty or full of herring or candlefish or shiners. All this told him what to think about tomorrow's fishing. With a clamshell, he scraped the blood-filled spinal channel and washed the salmon inside and out in salt water and laid it back in the fish box. Then he took the fish guts and rebaited the crab traps and loaded them back into the boat so John could reset them after lunch. Then my father washed his hands in the Sound, the last cleaning, the necessary attending done, and he and I walked the salmon box, one on each end, up to the cabin where my mother and John's wife, Helen, waited.

The next time I saw that fish was at dinner, the salmon fillets baked or roasted, the clams steamed open, the crabs boiled, small potatoes and vegetables in a bowl, lemon, tartar sauce, melted butter, and an assortment of knives, forks, picks, and pliers to get to the heart of the matter. I had no idea how good this feast was. Still steamed that I had yet to catch a fish, "skunked" the word nobody mentioned, the dime back where it came from, I had rowed John's skiff out to the buoy after lunch, determined to catch something, tied off at the buoy, and jigged for hours with a hand line. My bait was the leftover herring. There had to be something on the bottom, and there was; I caught starfish, kelp, seaweed, dogfish, sea slugs, a too-small crab, sea urchins, a miniature sole, and then a bright orange rock cod I hauled up and netted, being careful of its spines. Here was my contribution. Rising from the depths, the rock cod had looked huge, a gaping mouth and round baffled eyes, but when I cleaned it with my jackknife back on shore, there wasn't much left: two skinny fillets that my mother generously wrapped in tinfoil and placed in the oven. No one asked at dinner why I didn't take a piece of salmon, or amid all the bustle of clams and cracked crab, bowls of spent shells and a wide platter of salmon, what it was there bubbling in its tinfoil on my plate, garnished with a slice of lemon and tomato and a little parsley.

Maybe if I worked harder, I thought, then I would be blessed. In his essay "Ancient Forests of the Far West," Gary Snyder wrote that in the Northwest "people love to do hard work together and to feel that work is real. . . . Knowing and enjoying the skills of our hands and our well-made tools is fundamental." How true at Hat Island. My father and John built by hand the boat that got us there. Sometimes I imagine how whole communities left Norway and Sweden and sailed to New York, and headed west to find land in Minnesota, or to live near Seattle, another Norway even farther west, where lakes stayed open all winter and rivers emptied into Puget Sound. In their mind's eye they had brought the image of seacoasts and the sweep of a bow. They knew how to lay a keel and cut the ribs and brace them. In his mind's eye, John had seen the curves in his boat before he started building. A kind man who laughed and swore in equal portions, John took fishing as seriously as his unparalleled finish carpentry. In boots, black baggy pants, a work shirt, and army-green suspenders—with his bald head and beak nose, his pipe a cauldron of embers that flew and burned his shirt, his wife's furniture, and the rugs—he would cut cedar planks freehand on his table saw and set them into the steam tube and fire the boiler. Hours later, my father and John would pluck out a limp cedar plank and clamp it against the ribs; one would hold the steel block behind the rib, and the other would drive the brass nails through until, striking the steel, they clenched back into oak. Then another plank lapped over the first, and so on, clinker-built—a Mukilteo boat, they called it. This is how my father said it was done.

When they weren't fishing those summer weekends, John and my father worked on the cabin. I thought it was a huge place, but it wasn't, of course. There was a storeroom in back where my brother and I slept, and a front room big enough for two double beds, a few chairs, a four-burner wood stove, an alcove with a built-in table and benches, and a big front door with a brass knob, all surfaced with bark and driftwood. My mother and Helen, their hair covered in kerchiefs, stood on chairs and washed the knotty-pine walls with water and ammonia from a bucket. The smell drove me onto the porch, where I wrestled with jerry cans set in a row next to the ice-box and its foot-square block of ice we had brought in burlap over from the mainland. At the side of the cabin, my father and John stood over huge cedar logs, one propped up in the middle and leveled. These were storm drift, deadheads, refugees from a log raft perhaps. John and my father had peaveyed them up the beach last winter after a high tide. Using wedges and come-alongs, they had stored the logs behind the cabin to dry. Now, with a two-man cross-cut saw, they started to cut a two-foot piece off one end of the log.

Instructed to refill the jerry cans, I dragged them clanking to the skiff, pushed off, and rowed leisurely across Hat Island's small bay to where the catch barrels lay hidden. Runoff from the top of the island, filtered through sand cliffs and clay, the water filled huge wooden barrels I had to hike to get to. The trip over was easy, but I suffered on the way back, the cans now five gallons full and nearly fifty pounds apiece, the steps back to the beach slippery, the round beach stones kelp covered, the wind up and in my face. It was my job to return the skiff, secure it, and haul those cans one at a time back up through sand and driftwood and over logs, and set them full on the porch. It hurt. A necessary pain, I told myself, and a contribution to the common labor here, which seemed to last all afternoon at the cabin—the preparation, the food and dishes, the wood to be chopped and kindling split, the mending and splicing and arranging, engines and fishing gear to tend to, the cabin's stove always, and the odious lime-doused outhouse.

After stowing the jerry cans on the porch, I asked my mother what else I could do, and she said, "Go on now; I'll think of something later," which freed me to wander around the island if the tide were low enough, to sit on the point and watch for orcas or pilot whales, to pitch stones I found in the abandoned gravel quarry at the far side of the island.

By the time I wandered back, my father and John had cut the logs into two-foot sections and stacked several on end. Then John set a long, thick knife, its handles perpendicular to the blade—a "froe" I learned from reading Snyder—sharp edge down on the flat, and my father took a hammer and struck the thick edge of the knife and drove it ringing clear into the cedar. Then both of them braced the round with one hand and pulled on the froe handles with the other, and off popped a piece of cedar. Half an inch thick and the next wider as they split toward the center of the log, each piece was smooth-edged and rough-faced. I would stack them by the cabin next to rolls of tarpaper we had brought over in the boat. My father and John worked all afternoon. By the end of summer they hoped to have enough shakes to reroof the cabin, and maybe enough to cover an exterior wall or two. That night, the storeroom redolent with cedar, I lay awake and tried to calculate how many jerry cans filled and how many cedar shakes stacked and bound with cord might equal one salmon. I struggled with that old issue of good works, fearing nothing I did or could do would lift me into the elect.

That fear sharpened through two more summers. I wish I could say I suffered the wait gracefully. Even my father began to lose patience the August we drove to Sekiu for a three-day weekend—John and Helen in one rented cabin, and my father, mother, younger brother, and I in another. The first day, my father took my brother and me fishing in the sixteen-foot rented boat, trolling back and forth parallel to the shore. The fifteen-horse Evinrude we used was my father's, which he kept mounted like a trophy all year on a two-by-four brace in the garage at home.

My brother spent whole afternoons in the garage, twisting that throttle handle and making engine noises. Now he had a chance at the real thing and pestered my father to let him steer. "No, there are too many boats out here. Maybe later," my father said. I was seated in the bow, my rod as hypnotic in its wave rhythms as it had been for years. Several years younger than me and never keen on fishing, my brother fidgeted, tangled his line, lay back, turned over, stirred the herring bucket with his fingers, faced the other way, whined about his fate, and asked again and again until my father finally said, "OK. Pick up. We've got to move anyway.

"You sit here," he told my brother, pointing to the seat next to the idling Evinrude. "Steer toward the landslide. Take it easy. Make sure you give these boats out here a wide berth. They've all got lines out."

Maybe my brother didn't understand what "berth" meant. Maybe he was just too heavy-handed and unlucky, turning the throttle full so we jumped forward, our aluminum kicker boat leaping onto plane. Of course the fisherman seated in the first boat we crossed behind immediately grabbed his doubled-over rod, line screaming out of the reel at the same speed we were planing by.

"Stop, stop," my father said, grabbing the throttle. We settled quickly. Moving back to his middle seat, my brother got that *I'm-going-to-get-it* look on his face, tinged with red around his ears. Thankful this had nothing to do with me, I imagined an elaborate prop-tangled, nylon bird's nest. My father cut the Evinrude, methodically tipped it up, and locked it in place. From the bow I could see him reaching toward the prop, and when he sat back up, he had, to my surprise, the fisherman's line in his left hand and the hook in his right. "Here it is," he said over the water. "The hook just caught the skid. I'm sorry. It looks OK." And he held up the line and hook, a kind of offering and apology to that fisherman who stood at the back of his boat not twenty yards away.

And then the fisherman—a full-grown man, I remember—said, "Not OK by me. Thanks a hell of a lot, buddy." That tone, a cross between sarcasm and a sneer, I had heard many times on the playground battlefields of school, but never directed by another man toward my father, whose face tightened at once. He dropped the hook and line into the water.

Then he stood in our boat and pointed his finger and used a voice I'd not heard before, one very easy to hear across the water. "Keep it up, pal, and you'll be chasing your head down the street." It was absolutely convincing. Hair-raising and heart-thumping. Sekiu was not a very big place, maybe two streets, and I think that fisherman, who said nothing more and sat right down, knew it. I knew I had witnessed a line being crossed. Was this the world I so wanted to enter? My father's threat scared me. Suddenly this was not the same fishing trip. This one seemed serious. It was time to wake up.

I tried to pay closer attention through the second day of nothing, and all morning and afternoon of the third and last day, as John and my father and I trolled back and forth. My brother chose to stay onshore. Or the choice was made for him. I don't know. I know there was no dime on the seat this time. Both my father and John had caught a few small cohos, shaking hands after each fish, rebaiting the hooks, and grinning. But I didn't join in, envious and not a little desperate. I tried not to show it, adjusting my bait, thinking it was flawed or misshapen, or asking my father to check its action, or stripping too much line out and winding it in again, and asking my father to rebait my hooks again and again until I could tell by the silence I was testing his limits. Late in the afternoon he told John, who was steering, "Maybe one more pass down to the slide and back and then we'll head home."

Maybe it was simply resignation and hope at the same time. I imagined the long drive back to Seattle, empty-handed, and stripped out ten more feet of line as we trolled slowly against the current, the bay growing larger. I didn't want to leave. The line hummed and the bait worked deep. "Fish, fish," I said under my breath as my father did unconsciously, stripping out line three yards and winding up one, his last adjustment before sitting back to wait. Maybe it was the realization that all we do in a small boat could very well come to nothing, and we fish anyway. I remember my father saying once that the Olympic Peninsula had everything he ever wanted in life except work. Maybe I understood then a little of his frustration and how hard he had to work to get here, and that some days simply being in such a place, three hundred yards off Sekiu, afloat between the sea and sky, was catch enough.

Because at that moment something took hold. Suddenly the tip of my rod dove back and down toward the sea—not so much a pull as an anchor, a dead stop at the end of my line while we still trolled—my rod bent ninety degrees, and the line zipping out a foot at a time in rhythmic bursts. "You've got bottom," my father said. John shifted the engine to neutral.

"No, it's a fish," I said out of wishing. But when the line started to wander, and something deep shook so I felt it in my hands, I was suddenly afraid that what I wished for might be true. The butt of the rod in my stomach and my left hand above the reel, I dropped the rod toward the water, winding fast at the same time, and then lifted slow and steady. Drop and wind and lift, the routine I had imagined for years. If I had any twinge of doubt then, it was because the heaviness at the end of my line seemed to rise too easily toward the surface. Maybe kelp, I thought, or a deadhead. I couldn't see. Both hands on the gunwale, my father looked down into the water as I wound, my arms already growing tired.

Then he said, "Oh, Jesus," his eyes wide and mouth open. I saw him kick the bait bucket over. His baseball hat fell off. I saw him look at me and heard him say, "Fish," exactly the moment my fish panicked. The rod doubled hard and I hung on with both hands, the line zinging out, spraying water back and forth off the reel, the spool diameter shrinking fast. "No slack. Keep the tip up. Point the rod out the bow toward the line and we'll follow," he said to me. "Keep the rod up. Don't touch that drag. No slack. Keep winding. That's it. That's it."

By this time, John had the Evinrude in gear and steered whichever way my rod pointed, not full speed but steady so I could take in line, my father watching, net in hand. But it was far too soon for that, I discovered. We followed run after run, each one headed north—Sekiu, the calm bay, and all the other drift boats falling behind. My arms burned. When the fish ran hard, I would hold the rod up with my right hand and let my left drop to rest and then change back to wind when the fish slowed or turned again, all the line I had wound back before—drop, wind, and pull; drop, wind, and pull—having vanished through the guides in a heartbeat.

I had yet to see the fish. All I could feel was the weight, and when I stopped again to rest, maybe thirty minutes after the chase had begun, my father said, "Tired? Do you want me to help?"

Part of me did. Aching all over, afraid to lose this fish, and afraid to catch it for the loss of something I wouldn't understand for years, I knew my father would take care of this if I asked him. But another part of me, more stubborn and excited and driven by pride, said, "No, no. I'm OK." I was hardly sure, though the runs had shortened up considerably. I kept winding. Then I felt the fish shake its head as if it were saying *no, no, no.* Then, over the edge, I saw a huge shadow magnified in green water six feet down, neither rising nor sounding. My hands shook. I held him against the rod and it bent double. Then he lay over once and silver flashed like sun up through the water and my father barked at John, "Here's the net. Whatever you do, don't miss him. Do *not* miss him." When I lifted and wound, the fish rose headfirst and thrashed a moment, and with two hands, John, pipe clenched in his teeth, dipped the net down and through and my father grabbed and the both of them lifted the huge king spasmodic and flapping into the boat.

UPS delivered the rod in late August. It is straight and clean. The note from Don says, "I hope you like it." The new wraps holding the guides are yellow silk with red borders. Between the guides, red silk wraps evenly define the spaces, one wrap between the guides on the butt section; two, two; then three and three; then two on the tip. The cork handle and the aluminum seat have been cleaned, the rod and wraps varnished lightly. On the butt section just above the handle, "C. C. McKean" is saved, next to the number "15-9,'" indicating a heavy-weight, nine-foot salmon rod.

It will not be fished again. I want to rest it on pegs on the wall. Split bamboo, guides, wrap, handle, reel, hook, line and leader, the strike and run all serve as metaphor and occasion. My fish story lies refinished, too, though not done. A good fish story leaves amendment room, and there are complications in mine, certainly, that need attention.

The fact that this rod, for example, was designed to kill. Fishermen and devotees of split bamboo, from Izaak Walton through George Parker Holden to Norman McLean and John Gierach, describe classic rods in such forthright language. Even though I mostly trout-fish now and practice catch and release, I still "stick these magnificent animals in the face," to quote my good fisherman friend from Calgary, Neil Jennings.

Forty-two years ago on the boat seat in front of me, I killed a huge king salmon with a fishing rod and a club. I thought I had arrived. When my father laid my salmon on the dock back in Sekiu, a small crowd gathered in admiration. I boasted and preened: "That's mine. I caught that. Big fight."

Breaking the rods down and without looking at me, my father said, "Go ahead, lift it up to the scale." Hanging from a beam beside the cleaning sink, the butcher's scale and hook waited at eye level. Full of myself, I knelt beside the fish, fat and over a yard long, slipped two fingers beneath the gill plate, and lifted. Nowhere. Four fingers; then with two hands, one on each side, I finally got the dead weight of that fish up off the dock and strained—everyone quiet now and watching—toward the scale's hook, breathing harder and bending my knees. Terrified and embarrassed that I might not make it, I pushed and strained and groaned out loud just as the hook caught the gill plate, and the scale's needle oscillated wildly back and forth and settled finally on thirty-six pounds.

Without asking me first, my father and John cleaned the fish. It would feed us all. Most likely my father suggested that I had other necessary things to attend to: modesty and deference, for example, or a thought given to praise and words for such, each fish caught more gift than conquest. "He held on, sure did, and we chased that king halfway to Vancouver Island," my father said every time he told this fish story, the "he" reference always a little ambiguous.

I still fish for salmon, though infrequently, and observe my limit, and clean and eat what I catch. It feeds me in many ways. And for that I'm obliged to make amends. It's what I owe. This feeling has been especially acute since I saw a short film at the MK Nature Center in Boise, Idaho. In Caldwell to teach a "Writing and Nature" workshop a few summers ago, I took a field trip with my class to Boise to look at the center's re-creation of a trout stream. The most telling display, however, was that film, which shows how the construction in 1958 of the Oxbow Dam on the Snake River blocked the salmon run. The scene is devastating. There is no river left below the dam for all the salmon dead-ended. What were the builders thinking? Workers, desperate, awash in silver, dip salmon out and into buckets and containers to lift up and over the new dam, but it's hopeless, a thimble to bail the sea. This isn't husbanding a resource. Peter Matthiessen writes that such a dam is "another notable example of human progress gone awry."

What a horrifying waste—power or control the only payoff for a dam that kills salmon as surely as unscrupulous gillnetters kill a spawning stream by setting their nets across the mouth. An old, venerated run silenced once and for all.

Looking at my own requisite photograph, I'm sad and filled with mixed feelings for what's been lost over time: my father and Helen and John Carlson, those innocent and sleepy days adrift at Hat Island, a time "forever fled." Helen took the photo and framed it for me. I'm twelve, my North-City Merchants Little League baseball hat in my right hand, and two fingers of my left hand tucked into the gills of my huge king salmon. Hanging from the scales, it's nearly as long as I am, head to just above my knees.

The dyes in the old Kodak print have faded over the years, so that day on the dock in Sekiu looks washed out, too full of light. The fish is silver and symmetrical. I remember now, the coat I'm wearing in this photo is my mother's. Worried about the cold, she zipped her down coat up around my neck as we left in the morning, but this was the last time I would wear it. Maybe this was the last day for that boy to be a boy, smiling, awake now, the moment his—August 12, 1958—after which obligations and work and consequence struck hard in deep, endless runs.

SEVEN-STEP PROCEDURE

IN OUR LIVING ROOM MARV HARSHMAN, THE HEAD BASKETBALL coach for Washington State University, talked to my mother and grandmother. My high school graduation was a month away. I was a tall, skinny prospect who had scored enough points my senior year to attract attention. Recruited by in-state colleges, I should have felt flattered, but the more schools that called, the greater my hesitation. I stalled. Even my mother wrung her hands and turned up the heat.

It was as if at seventeen I needed a script for my life, a how-to manual, a little book with all the answers. I remember when I was very young asking my father what the names were for places between the towns. Somehow the absence between names—a wilderness of sorts, unaccounted for and infinite—felt intimidating. They were lost places, the unknown, where I might lose myself.

In the kitchen, out of earshot, my father asked me to think about the next four years. Would the scholarship still be there if I got hurt? What was expected between seasons?

When we gathered again in our living room, my grandmother in her rocking chair, we all considered Washington State's offer: a four-year, full-ride basketball scholarship. Sipping coffee from a china cup my mother reserved for holidays, a plate of cookies balanced on his knee, Coach Harshman explained that the scholarship was secure even in case of injuries, how each of his Washington State players was a student first and a basketball player second, how the athletic department would supervise our studies, provide tutors if need be, and make every effort to help its student-athletes succeed on the floor and in the classroom.

To the great relief of my mother, who had exhausted herself filing school brochures and fending off weeks of recruiters, coaches, and alumni on the phone, I signed up to be a Cougar. Coach Harshman even promised me a summer job to help me organize those vacant summer months between high school and college.

◦ ◦ ◦

IT WAS MY FIRST JOB, AND I WAS SURE IT WOULD PROVIDE A MAP and method. The Cougars had contacts in Tacoma. A few phone calls and three weeks after committing to Washington State, I stood at attention before the car hoist at the Standard station on South Tacoma Way in Tacoma, Washington. As Service Station Salesmen, Grade One, we recruits learned that service was our goal and the Seven-Step Procedure our means. Look sharp. Be neat. Hurry up. You are the steps. Service now and here's how.

This was more like it. Here was my script, my summer playbook. My only worry was that the standard-issue uniform for Service Station Salesmen—white pants, starched white shirt, black shoes, a black belt, a black bow tie and a starched white cap—came in only three sizes, the largest of which fell ten inches too short for future Pac-8 basketball centers. Undaunted, my mother sewed tails on my shirts and let down the pants and thought my black Converse high-tops would be OK. Although my enthusiasm was as starched as my untucked shirt, the car hoist stood in the way, its full reach somewhere around my shoulders. I knew I would never keep the hat clean.

As if the burden of orchestrating my future had been lifted, I wanted to please everyone: my customers, my future coaches, and Standard Oil, who had given me this job with its neat and tidy procedures. I had seven steps to face the day. No Army to worry about. No war in Southeast Asia. No riot police and broken cities. No life of pickup games or late-night pool after eight hours of shoveling asphalt.

What did I know? "O youth!" Joseph Conrad says over and over in his story "Youth: A Narrative," as if that refrain and a shake of the head explain it all. Ready for a "full-service" answer, I was seventeen in a stunned world, happy to have a plan and a too-small hat. Step by step through the summer, however, I discovered that my hat was the least of my problems.

° ° °

STEP ONE. *The greeting: "Good morning" (afternoon, evening, using name if known).*

As bright as bleached linen, we new recruits rushed to the cars in good cheer and welcome. What they didn't tell us was to pay attention before that window rolled down. At my first posting, I can still see the car coming late at night, the bars just closing, and here my customer turns off the main highway onto the road next to our station, and then in a wide arc onto the blacktop that leads to our pumps.

"Watch this," Harry, the old manager, said, stubbing out his smoke and taking a step back into the office. At the ready, I watched from the door, a foot lifted to serve, but a tug at the back of my shirt held me up just long enough as the car lights swept the building next to our station, then the service bay, and finally arrived, the big sweeping fender of the car not slowing down. As if a kid drew an arc too big, his compass off the paper onto the desk, the car crushed the racks of oil cans next to our office, creased the metal siding beneath the window, plopped down off the sidewalk, and hiccupped to a stop at a forty-five-degree angle next to the regular pump. "Now," Harry said.

I stepped up to the car, knocked on the driver's window, which wandered down, and into the anonymous haze I said, "Good evening."

This was not the only type of bad aim. The wide-arc approach, wind-aided, proved the most dangerous to the service-station salesman crew, but the too-shallow approach was more common. Before stations provided breakaway hoses, the pumps stood at serious risk. These events usually took place early in the morning, the police officer on his way to duty at 5:30 perhaps the best example. He was moving only at a crawl, but somehow his front bumper caught the hose on the first pump. Unfortunately, he wanted gas from the last pump in his line of sight. I don't understand why he didn't hear the first pump ripping out of its bolts, falling into pump number two, the high test, and then dragging ten feet like a tin can tied to a wedding limousine.

"Good morning," I said.

Eventually my "greeting" served less as a welcome and more as a trial run. Windows rolled down on mastiffs—or worse, schnauzers—or the mysteriously naked, or a bank of smoke first and then questions about the nature of the universe and how to get to McDonald's or Topeka. Sometimes grunts and shrugs. Sometimes the door opened up so fast I needed to dance away, the sprinting driver desperate, "Where's the can?" Over the course of that summer, there must have been a thousand cordial responses to my greeting, but what I remember most is the swearing from the dark interior of a '57 Ford station wagon late one night.

"Good evening," I said, and before the driver, a young boy, could say a word, his passenger called me an asshole and a son of a bitch, and explained how I was gonna get my ass kicked. From the driver's open mouth came no sound.

° ° °

STEP TWO. *Gasoline sale: "Do you wish your tank filled? Do you use Chevron Supreme or Regular?" Confirm gas order: "Thank you. Fill your tank with Supreme," or whatever the specific order actually is, dollars or gallons.*

I discovered there's a reason for confirmation. One night I was certain the young and charming customer driving for her mother said "Fill it with regular." Maybe I was tired. Maybe I paid too much attention to her smile or adjusting my bow tie or tucking the tail of my shirt in with one hand, the other resting on the car roof as I leaned closer to see her, wondering whether or not I should tell her about my playing basketball for the Cougars and how Coach Harshman had signed that letter right in front of us. Maybe I was just naive, for after I filled her tank, I asked her for $6.50, and she said she only wanted $2.00 worth.

"No. You said fill it with regular."

"I said two dollars."

Ah, thus the letter of Step Two. The manual said nothing about charm or the lack of it, or misguided self-impressions, or what to do in such an unusual case. I don't think she would have cared about the Cougars. Here in my second week of front-line graveyard service-station duty, I wanted to do the right thing. Step Two says double check. I didn't. My fault. In thinking back, I shouldn't have drained her tank, guessing how many gallons would equal

$4.50. Though she drove into the garage, they wouldn't get out of their car. Still, I shouldn't have hoisted them up, the two faces grim and silent in the windows as the steel piston lifted them to the ceiling. And maybe unscrewing the drain plug, the gas spilling, and filling bucket after bucket wasn't accepted procedure. Twenty minutes later I had my fifteen gallons. Not smart. But I was almost eighteen and red-faced with pride.

The boy's face in the darkened Ford station wagon keeps coming back to mind. He asked for five dollars of regular, though he had to repeat it over the cursing coming from the passenger side. I was an idiot and contemptible and a shit. "Five dollars of Chevron regular it is," I said, suddenly frightened enough to forget the next step.

° ° °

STEP THREE. *Under-hood service.*

Our training taught us neat and tidy visual inspections. How to pull the dipstick, wipe it clean, insert the stick once again for an accurate read, and then to walk it back to our customer, the "full" to "add oil" scale held above a clean rag for their inspection. Look at belts, filters, etc., for preservation of the customer's safe journey and well-being. At least, that was the noble intention.

In practice, homage was paid to the "accessories list." Sales led to good graces and transfer up. As well as shame. Fan belts, air filters, thermostats, and radiator caps; brake-light bulbs and, on good days, U-joints and wheel bearings; and the prize for all aspiring Service Station Salesmen who covet Grade Two, a tire sale. The list hung on a clipboard above the office desk for all to see, station managers and salesmen alike. If you had a sale, wiper blades for example, you could take the clipboard down, flip the pages (deliberately running your finger down the column until you found a blank space), click your pen a few times, and write in the date, the product, the number, and your initials. The pose and the click of the pen seemed crucial.

The sale itself was far more theatrical. The opening complication for rookies like me was finding the latch to the hood. The next was the artful shake of the head, the driver looking out his window now wondering, of course, why you are peering into the ticking recesses of his engine compartment. Grab your chin. "Tsk" if possible. Call another salesperson over and shake your head again and whisper and point, and then reach down into the darkness as your partner tips his hat back and whistles. This works best for an out-of-state-licensed car, with three combustible kids in the back seat, suitcases stuffed in the trunk or lashed to the roof, and maps, compasses, red pencils, and fast-food debris littering the dashboard, the floor, and the door pockets.

"See this fan belt—How far did you say you were going?—those cracks here on the inside, and if she disintegrates, well then, there goes your water pump and generator, and that battery looks like it's leaking but should hold, especially if you don't have to depend on it."

Engines choke to death from clogged filters, no air, and tainted gas, and it always happens in the middle of a desert or mountain range, hundreds of miles from salvation. Belts let fly and tires go flat. All your bulbs burn out beneath a new moon on a dirt road ten miles south of the border. Wheel bearings freeze. Wipers blades shred and layer the dirt on your windshield like impasto. Yes, yes. An ounce of prevention. What would Ben Franklin have said if he had had a car? No pay, no gain?

By this time, Mr. Traveler slides out from behind the wheel to peer in at the mysteries beneath his hood. Turn the belts up and bend them. Fiddle the gasket on the radiator cap. Shine that high-tech bulb through the air filter; if you can't see light, there's trouble ahead. A few customers, terrified by the unknown, said OK. Change it all. Others suspected a squeeze and said forget it. I never pressed the issue, but still felt mixed the whole time, being a rookie at the accessories list and more than a little astonished at the full-time real practitioners of the "procedure." Some might call it "the fleece." But I don't remember a sale that wasn't necessary, or wouldn't be eventually. Maybe I was simply on my way to being a true Service Station Salesman who believed his own pitch. Maybe I found too much comfort in the seven steps.

One man in particular agreed to let the pros move his car from the outside bays inside to the hoist. Once the hydraulics of that operation pressured up, a great deal was lifted, including a large share of the man's latest paycheck. An Army sergeant from Fort Lewis, ten miles south of our station, he obviously loved his beautiful 1956, two-door, blue Chevy Impala. I stood back in admiration and horror as Frank, the assistant manager, and Bud, a Service Station Salesman with rank, started up on him. Don't buy in, I thought to myself. Don't listen. But I said nothing, and really had nothing to say when Bud expressed his sympathy and admiration. Frank shook the sergeant's hand, an act of partnership in fine cars. Their concern was platonic, of course, the car near perfection already, only the polish rag needed and, of course, new U-joints. For you see how much slack exists in the drive shaft, and this means new bushings, and oh, the tread on these tires has worn unevenly which means the ball joints and zirk fittings and wheel bearings lie worn and leaking.

Though my suspicion lingered, what did I know? These veteran salesmen were specialists. The sergeant offered no argument against the need for maintenance, a belief he probably championed himself. In fatigues and shiny boots, he smoked and paced outside the station as if his car were expecting. I also have to admit that the '56 Chevy was more beautiful as it descended from hours on the heavenly hoist, new wiper blades, the drivetrain tightened to perfection, four new tires squeaking as he backed slowly out of our station, all his windows and lights bright and shining.

° ° °

STEP FOUR. *Windshield service: Clean front and rear windows, wind wings, side mirrors, and if time permits, clean side windows and headlight and taillight lenses. Be sure to check windshield-wiper condition.*

As trainees that first week, we even volunteered to wash the inside of a car's windows. This proved so bothersome and awkward, especially when the driver and his passenger stayed seated in the car, that we dropped that offer as soon as our instructor took a break.

What we kept was the "energy and enthusiasm maneuver," as follows: Standing next to the driver's side, spray the windshield with fluid. With your left hand and paper towels wipe the windshield clean, standing upright and next to the car. At the same time, place your right hand, elbow held at your side, against the top of the driver's door where it seals against the roof, and push rhythmically as you wipe the windshield with your left hand. Push hard. Rock that car. The gentleman, on his way to church perhaps, his tie swaying back and forth, will return another day, convinced of your enthusiasm and devotion to cleanliness, though his wife rocking in the seat next to him, the sun visor and its mirror down, won't get her lipstick on straight.

The state patrolman in his Ford wouldn't settle for enthusiasm. Invariably he would stop by at two in the morning to get his windshield cleaned, pointing from the inside at each smear and bug carcass. *Now?* I'd motion. *OK?* But he would find another gnat or oil spot, and I would wipe away five more minutes. In the end, I didn't mind his fussiness or his assuming I was responsible for his windshield and his tires.

° ° °

STEP FIVE. *Tire service: Check pressure with pressure gauge and condition (visual) of all tires, including spare if customer allows.*

In 1964, the tires on police cars had an inner tire and outer tire all in one, a hedge against high-speed blowouts. After I had scoured the state patrolman's windshield, he handed me a tire needle so I might check the inner tire pressure on all his tires, then the outer with my tire gauge. Once his car was pressured, cleaned, filled, and wiped, he would pay with a credit card, once thrown out the window at me when he saw a speeder and couldn't wait. "I'll be back," he yelled, hitting the sirens and lights as I picked up the credit card he had just run over.

As that summer progressed, I grew to appreciate the state patrolmen and the sheriff, who on occasion squawked at me on his car's PA when he found me nodding off at four in the morning behind the office window. When sent out to change a tire on the freeway, I invariably found the car parked just on the shoulder, semis in the outside lane compressing the air in front of them and trailing a vacuum, the flat I had to fix (the outside rear, of course) eight inches away from twenty tons traveling at seventy, the air pounding me against the car and then sucking at my shirt as the Doppler pitch dropped and another one of my starched hats flew down the freeway like a leaf in a storm. If the state patrolman was in the neighborhood, he would wedge his car behind me on the shoulder and turn his lights on and sit there until I finished.

Sometimes the sheriff simply drove through two or three times a night as I suffered through graveyard by myself. The shift is aptly named. There is a Gahan Wilson cartoon showing Batman, an alien with ten arms, two hobos, and a werewolf standing in line at an all-night store, and it wasn't until I worked graveyard at the Standard station on the freeway south of Tacoma that I realized these were the regular customers. The Mercedes with the nervous and painted girls. The woman who couldn't explain the vibration in her car until she remembered she had run into a bridge just a few miles back. The skaters, nozzle left on the ground. The junk collectors, their station wagons portable yard sales—so full of newspaper and cans and detritus, only the driver had room to look up at me over phone books through the cracked windshield. There was the full-blown, chopped and raked, slick-tired, Holley carburetor, four-on-the-floor street burner, and its pompadoured, sleeve-rolled, Camel-smoking driver who wanted a buck's worth of high-test. The four-door, black-walled, in-line six-cylinder Rambler. The rust buckets and the white-sidewalled, rolled, pleated, and chromed two-toned and TV-equipped Cadillacs. All the mysterious cars, smoke-filled, with their sullen passengers—or tired or pissed or lost.

I remember especially the three young soldiers from Fort Lewis on a Saturday night about 10:30, let loose from basic training. From the deep South by their accents, they seemed more than anxious to hit the town. "Where's a bar. We just got a pass. We're headed out next month so we're going to celebrate." Whoever issued their pass at 10:00 P.M. on a Saturday night, maybe the sergeant with the Impala, had a cruel streak.

"Where are you from?" I asked.

"Alabama," one said.

"Well, you'd better hurry. This is Washington State. Home of the blue laws. Bars close on Saturday night at twelve."

The early-morning air always felt weird in Tacoma, ripe with odors from the pulp mill if the wind blew south, and more than a little threatening as single cars, maybe a headlight out, exited the freeway and wandered slowly into the station at 3:30. As the summer waned, I worried more and more about working alone on the graveyard shift. When I asked what to do in case of a holdup, the station manager said, "Don't worry. Just give them everything. Offer to take the register out to their car." Hey, I thought, this was service taken to the extreme. Where was the procedure?

The attendant at the Texaco across the street advocated a strategy even less comforting—a snub-nosed thirty-eight revolver kept in his desk drawer. Sometimes we would cut the late-night boredom by talking at the edge of his station or mine. "Wanna see my answer to robbery?" he asked once, and looking over his shoulder to watch for the sheriff, took the revolver out of his pocket and handed it to me. I held it up to the light and turned the cylinder to see the copper domes, and shivered for the weight and cold.

° ° °

STEP SIX. *Collection: Complete filling the tank, replace nozzle in pump, note the gallons and amount of sale. Return to the customer, always approaching from the front.*

By the end of the summer I wanted to add, "keeping hands up and in plain sight." I would tally the oil sale, any accessories if I scored there, note the number of gallons to the tenth, take a deep breath, and approach the driver's-side window. A charge was easy. The assortment of denominations—nickels, dimes, bus tokens, postage stamps, Canadian bills, the Italian lire once I couldn't accept—was more problematic. With my hands full of change, I would manage to unlock the cash box set outside by the pumps, distribute my change, and lock things back up.

But a customer not mentioned in my seven-step guide to perfect service sorely tested my collection skills one day. "Can you change this?" he asked after his two-dollars worth of gas, pulling a fifty-dollar bill from a wad of bills in his hand. "I need two twenties and a ten." So I counted out two twenties and a ten, plus eight because two for the gas from ten, and held them, thinking *wait a minute.*

"Oh, yeah, sorry," he said. "What I really need is two twenties, and maybe you can give me a ten for a bunch of ones. Here, I'll count it for you." But that seemed unwise, standing there as I was, the cash box open, key in the lock and tied to my belt, a fifty in one hand and change in the other.

"That's OK. Let me," I said, and I stacked two twenties and a five and three ones in his hand.

"I've got a mess of ones now. Would you mind giving me a ten-dollar bill for ten ones?" and he counted out the ones and I handed him a ten and he turned back toward his car and stopped. "Pardon me," he said, "I think I screwed up. Did I give you a ten in all those ones?"

Sure enough. When I looked in the ones slot in the cash box, there was a ten-dollar bill beneath nine ones. "Well, I've got another single," he said. "What I gave you adds up to nineteen, one more makes twenty, so just give me a twenty-dollar bill and we're even."

Now I wasn't sure at all. Suddenly, the whole summer seemed confusing. I plucked a twenty out of its slot and held it up in one hand and took his one-dollar bill with the other. My hat started to tilt and the voice in my head said *this isn't adding up but don't ask me how.* So out of panic and confusion I locked all the money in the box and yanked the key out by its tether.

"Hey, where's my twenty?"

"OK," I said, opening the box. "Here's the mistaken ten you gave me plus the one which makes eleven dollars back which is one more than you asked for originally but I'm willing to sacrifice," and shut the box as a patrol car drove into the bay and the service bell started ringing.

Or at least I think that's what I did. By that time both of us were baffled, scratching our heads. He turned the bills over and looked out the corner of his eye at the police car. I moved toward the paper-towel dispenser, the patrolman searching his window for something I might clean. Maybe I was the one who got cleaned. I know now I was the mark in a "change snafu" attempt. My quick-change artist must have thought a quick exit prudent, and my need to get away from him was so great I even forgot an important part of Step Six: offer a Chevron credit-card application.

I was young and hurt that someone tried to steal from me, even more disillusioned by the con artist than by those customers who wanted to beat me to a pulp. The boy in the Ford station wagon comes to mind again. When I asked for the five dollars for gas, and would he like an application for a credit card, the voice in the darkness went spasmodic, guttural, laced with cursing. Then, on the far side of the car, the passenger door kicked open. My heart thumped. I had not seen hatred like this before, the tenor of his cursing and threats and bluster my absolute doom. Maybe he worked for Standard Oil. Maybe my just turning eighteen with an untucked shirt, grease-stained pants, a Standard hat no longer white from so many grease-covered and dirt-lathered undercarriages stood for something this man hated, for here he was out of the dark, coming around the end of the car, wheeling, and oh, my . . .

He was ancient and skinny and absolutely pickled. His first right cross originated years ago, and he was still throwing it, fist at slow motion and the rest of his arm, shoulder, and body following all the way to the ground. The air proved too thick. He swatted at flies, cursed me as I backed toward the station, his left and right combinations at my belt level as slow as the tide. With the oil rag wadded in my hand, I held him at bay, touching his forehead once to measure our distance and asking the boy, who had gotten out of the car to follow us, to help me. "Who is this guy? Can you get him away from me?" I asked.

"My grandfather," he said. "He's been drinking. I need you to help me get him back into the car."

"Tell him to stop swinging or I'll hurt him." I didn't mean this and knew it. But just then in my life I knew I could hurt him, knew that given the fear—for I was very afraid of this old man's utter contempt for me—and the anger that follows, I could hit him. Here was the dilemma. Age gave him authority. I had learned from my father that authority deserved respect. But this man wanted to hurt me. Suddenly I was tired of working graveyard, tired of the hostility and insolence, tired of the swindle, tired of being invisible in my uniform and starched hat. I hated the way my own anger felt. Pro-basketball scouting reports, years later, said I was too small to be a center—a "tweener," and not mean enough. Yes, true even back at the Standard station.

That night beside the pumps, all I wanted was to steer this old man out of my existence. His grandson and I bumped and nudged him in a big circle back toward the passenger side of the Ford station wagon—he was still swinging and cursing—lined him up, and with one final roundhouse he threw himself into the passenger seat and we slammed the door. I collected my five dollars, but the kid drove off so quickly we never exchanged another word.

° ° °

STEP SEVEN. *Thanks and invitation to return.*

By August, I was anxious for school to begin at Washington State University. I hadn't said much to the station manager or the other guys working at the station, or seen much of them for that matter. Given my graveyard duty, I think they knew I wasn't long for this line of work. I mentioned the Cougars only in passing, and in three months no one asked about my going to school. Who was I to think better of myself? I kept my mouth shut, as my father recommended, and did the job—well enough, I thought, to get me through August and onto the basketball court in Pullman.

There was one customer in particular, however, that best defined my Standard Oil career. The problem was that by August I thought I knew what I was doing, thought for a moment I was a true Service Station Salesman Grade One, an error Huxley might explain as mistaking a symbol for the thing it stands for.

An accessories-list dream, my customer asked if I might service his new pickup-with-camper because he was on the road for the last part of August and all of September. His Chevy truck was a thing of beauty—tended, washed, polished, detailed, and pampered. Not a dust speck. Not a loose piece of paper. The camper was so tall, I had to pull the service-bay door up with the haul rope higher than usual for him to inch his truck over the hoist, which could only lift his truck a couple of feet before the camper touched the ceiling.

But three feet was enough. On my knees, I lubed and oiled and changed belts and checked seals and wiped and tested brakes and U-joints and caps and batteries. All the while, this man stood in the office watching through the window. He wrung his hands and looked worried while his wife patted his shoulder every once in a while before she finally sat down in the office and read an old issue of *Motor Week.*

Not to worry. The man wanted his car serviced. I could do that. I tightened the bolts and polished his windows and, finally, bowed to him at the finish and presented him with what I thought was a comprehensive but fair bill.

"On the card? Thank you. Yes, the belts were OK, but you needed a new A-17 paper-composite air filter and new wiper blades, which we had in stock, so I went ahead and put those on.

Your truck took six quarts of 10-30 Standard oil, and I filled the wiper-fluid tank and topped off your radiator and greased the fittings. Your U-joints look OK. Transmission OK, differential OK. I hope you have a nice vacation." I rattled on with the Standard patois.

He looked relieved. The patient had survived—or so we thought—and I stood in front of his truck, motioning as if I were directing traffic, as he backed it out of the bay slowly, looking back and forth in his mirrors, nervous that he might ding the sides of his truck.

Then the scraping, I couldn't tell from where. And then a sick feeling. Then from the top of his elegant and shiny camper, over the front and past his spotlessly clean windshield, past his very eyes, all the vents and aluminum trap doors and spigot pipes that had adorned the top of his fine camper clattered and banged onto his shiny, polished hood, spun around, and fell one by one onto the floor.

Then I remembered the garage door. It had fallen low enough to scrape the top of his camper as cleanly as a new grader blade. At that moment I resigned my Standard career. I was not cut out for this. He was a kind man and stunned nearly to tears, his wife pointing out where to fill in the Standard Service Station accident and claim forms I found after rummaging through the desk.

"I'm sorry," I said, and thought about telling him this wasn't really my line of work, that I was going to be a Cougar and play for Coach Harshman in Pullman, Washington. But all that mattered to my customer was that his truck had suffered damage. If you wear the hat, it's your line of work, my father would have said. So I said sorry again and filled out the forms and thought of what the company might do. Silently to myself, I praised the day I would leave for school. I had had enough.

When the district manager showed up the next day, I explained my mistake. Thumbing through the accessories list, he said, "These things happen," and "Think about us after school because you have a future with this company."

A future? I thought about it. I also thought how pleased I was going to be in Pullman at our first basketball team meeting, how the public served up more than the Seven Steps could handle, and how glad I was that I was no longer seventeen.

By early September, my student-athlete career had begun—my new teammates, veterans joking among themselves and rookies, all settling in their chairs, and the coaches walking in dressed in WSU sweats, whistles around their necks. "For you freshmen," Coach Harshman began, "I'd like to say welcome and pay attention. The season begins now, despite what the schedule might say. And one other thing. When we talked to you new recruits last spring, we said that you would be a student first and an athlete second. Well, we lied. Your work on the court is first and foremost. Dedication and desire are your tools. The game begins now."

So much for recruitment promises and noblesse oblige. "Full service," I said to myself, and looked around. No one heard me, and no one seemed surprised.

PLAYING FOR JUD

FROM HIGH IN THE STANDS, JUD HEATHCOTE LOOKED TORTURED, a tragic figure in a grand opera, so self-consumed with sorrow or lamentation or anger that we feared what he might do to himself. His whining was a high tenor screech, and his posture crushed. The stories about him were commonplace enough to approach the mythic—how he slammed a basketball to the floor in anger only to have it bounce straight up and strike him in the nose, hunched over as he was in his half-bear, half-wrestler crouch; how he struck his own head with the heel of his hand in frustration, a kind of audible self-mutilation; how he ripped the top of his socks off in anger, or as some say in the optical illusion of retelling, how he lifted himself off the bench by his socks until the argyle gave way and he fell back into his chair and over. Back and forth, pacing, hands out to plead with the officials, his own players, the very fates themselves. All punctuated by his out-of-tune aria of injustice and bafflement.

Twenty years after playing for Jud, I rediscovered close up his precarious balance of calm and catastrophe. At Iowa's Carver-Hawkeye arena, Jud's Michigan State Spartans, then in first place in the Big Ten, were being overrun by the fast-breaking, seemingly undisciplined hometown Hawkeyes. The noise was at ear-damage level. Managers quickly set out folding chairs for a time-out huddle. Sweating and exhausted, the starters watched Jud pound his fist into his hand, as if it were a gavel calling this game to order. But his voice was exact and even, laying out strategy and offering encouragement, and all those fine players at Michigan State—Steve Smith, Mike Peplowski, Kirk Manns, Eric Snow, Shawn Respert, some all-American, some all–Big Ten—all those players listened.

I listened too. I remember how it felt. In the sixties I played for Jud and Marv Harshman at Washington State University. For more than twenty years, I have replayed those seasons over and over, the violence and pain and discipline and humor and anger, the wins and, of course, the losses. It was a classic education without books, corporal and exhausting. Sometimes I regret being so myopic during those turbulent years from 1964 to 1968. On campus, students protested, breaking from convention and authority and the war. I remember in 1968 feeling defensive about my letterman's jacket. "Establishment," someone sneered. "I'm cold," was my half-hearted response. The memories are complex and ambivalent, and then as simple as the ball in hand, the echo of its bouncing in an empty gym. Years later, as I sat behind the Michigan State bench, the memories drew close. I was family again, and from the first row could speak, with practice now, of family matters.

When I wrote Jud to tell him I was going to school in Iowa City and to ask if I could get tickets to the Michigan State game, he wrote back to say there would be tickets for me as long as I didn't root for those sons-a-bitches. When I picked the tickets up at will-call, they read "row 2, courtside." The usher pointed down the steps. The long descent felt nostalgic. Before sixteen thousand Iowa fans, we found our seats directly behind Jud. Beneath the lights, the game was intimate again, the floor crowded and tense. I had forgotten how much happens in so small a space, and how, Macbeth-like, the hand and mind act as one. I could hear the conversations again between the players themselves, clipped, single-word information—*left, right, switch, mine, my fault*—all directed to honing the moment to a simple edge, your two points and their absolute denial. And audible through the roar, the one voice the players on the floor heard was Jud's song *verismo,* full of signals, melancholy, directions, spleen, admonishments, and finally praise.

It's the praise I remember seeking. If I screwed up, I felt that I had let the coaches down, that this game meant everything to them. Returning to the bench, I knew I would hear about my failure in a mix of analysis and despair. If I did well, the encouragement would be there. Once when our Washington State team played the University of Washington at Hec Edmundson Pavilion, I heard two words spoken clearly in a crowd of ten thousand and the noisy rush of the game. Guarded by Jay Bond, Washington's center, whose strategy was to front me at my low-post position, leaning with his right arm folded against me and his left in front waving in the passing lane, I kept trying to move farther out so that our guard Lenny Allen at the top of the key could pass me the ball. Jay Bond kept inching farther and more aggressively in front. I would move out and so would he. Finally, I made a sudden move toward the ball, Lenny Allen pump-faked, Jay Bond scrambled to front, and I changed direction with two quick steps toward the basket, leaving Jay Bond all by himself. It was a backdoor, a classic move, though a rare event in my repertoire; Lenny laid the pass in just so, and all I had to do was rise and drop the ball in. All timing and a wonderful pass. As I ran under the basket and back down court, I heard Jud say, "Nice move." Ten thousand voices, and one clear in its weight and authority. The basket was worth two points, and praise I have never forgotten.

It took a long time to earn that praise. Gangly, awkward, and eager to play, I was recruited out of Wilson High School in Tacoma by Marv Harshman, the head basketball coach at Washington State, who explained in his handwritten letters how badly the Cougars needed me. The center position would be mine when I was a sophomore. I could get a fifth-year stipend if needed. They would throw in a pair of contact lenses. They were building the basketball program, and I could play a crucial role. He called me a "student-athlete." My parents were sold, as was I. Signing the letter of intent, I agreed to play for Marv Harshman, a gentleman, an all-American hero at Pacific Lutheran University in Tacoma, and now the head coach at a Pac-8 Division One school. I was ready for the big time.

◦ ◦ ◦

THE NEXT FALL, I HADN'T BEEN ON CAMPUS VERY LONG WHEN Coach Harshman introduced me to a slightly balding man who looked like Don Rickles. This was the new freshman basketball coach. I don't remember Jud saying much. His tone seemed perfunctory, as if he was unsure about me. He asked something about my being in shape and getting ready for the season. What struck me immediately was that the basketball office in Bohler Gym looked no bigger than my room at home, with no window shades and only two desks, one for Harshman and one for Bobo Brayton, the head baseball coach and substitute assistant basketball coach whose favorite expression was "That's as obvious as a horse turd in a pan of milk." They borrowed the secretary down the hall in the athletic director's office. Jud would be replacing Bobo. I wondered if they would share the desk.

But during the first week of practice, I had larger worries. After the first team meeting, when the coaches explained that basketball was our first priority at Washington State and they weren't going to let us forget it, the haranguing began. Many of us were freshmen, ex–high school stars, and even Pete, the irascible equipment manager, growled at us. Maybe I wasn't as ready for college ball as I thought I was. During the first week, I also discovered that Coach Harshman focused mainly on the varsity. As a freshman, I was really playing for Jud. I had never been treated like this before.

"What the hell is that? Take that damn Wilson High School turnaround stick shot and leave it in your high school drawer," Jud barked. "There's no way you can play at Washington State if . . ." and then followed an infinite number of transgressions to complete the sentence. Technical problems rated eyebrow-raising impatience and a short demonstration. More egregious errors, such as lack of hustle and stupid choices, earned serious upbraiding and questions that have no good answer: "When are you going to learn, son? What does it take? What do I have to do?"

As the year progressed, we learned to take cover. When the whistle shrieked in the middle of a drill, and you heard "No, no, no" or "Please, how many times . . . ," your first wish was that the scolding wasn't for you. In the Midwest, tornado sirens get the same effect. Everyone seems torn, looking up to see what's coming while heading down to the cellar to hide. We would wander to the edge of the court, shuffle, look at our feet, and catch our breath while the chosen one suffered. After a while, we played with a kind of running-scared and *oh-no* demeanor, which I have seen even on Jud's Michigan State teams. It's a *your-father-knows-you-broke-the-neighbor's-window* look; all that's left is the sentence, the long walk back to the bench, or Jud's bear-like shuffle-walk toward you for an explanation. In a *Sports Illustrated* article that celebrates his career, Jud admits that "Like Bobby [Knight] I'm a negative coach. I'm always harping on what's bad rather than praising what's good. Yes, I've hurt some kids, and I've been bad for some kids. But one thing I'm always proud of is that our players get *coached.* And I think most of them get better every year."

For the 1964–65 season, the Jud-coached freshman basketball team at Washington State had twenty-two wins and no losses. We were balanced and deep. The highest individual scoring average on the team was twelve points per game, and the entire team average was eighty-two. Freshman games at Bohler Gym in Pullman had always been the opening act for the varsity, the rookies with their hand-me-down uniforms and bad passes playing to empty stands. As the season progressed, however, interest in our team began to grow, and at the halfway point we were even getting statewide news coverage. The *Tacoma News Tribune* noted that "Washington State's freshmen own the state's longest collegiate winning streak—eleven straight. The Coubabes beat North Idaho JC 102-61 on Friday night, then came back Saturday to upend Columbia Basin 63-59 to snip the Hawks' victory string at thirty-seven in a row. Marv Harshman lauded the Coubabe-CBC game as the finest freshman basketball game he's ever seen. 'It wasn't run and shoot. It was just a real basketball game,' he said." I would add that it was a real game because of Jud's coaching. We played with a mix of desperation and pride. We wanted that clean record, and we wanted to stay in Jud's good graces. By the end of the season, our record and the rumor of the red-faced, hair-tearing, combustible freshman coach named Jud had filled the stands.

Those players who made the transition to the varsity team indeed got better the next year. Out of sixteen freshman players, six made the varsity team, but several of the best players on the freshman team decided not to play at all. Some dropped out of school for academic reasons. Others decided they couldn't survive another year of Jud. "How do you put up with all that yelling at you?" someone asked. I remember saying that I tried to listen to what he had to say but not necessarily how he said it, that he had good things to teach. I was young and deferential. It was 1965, and on campus, ROTC was still a major. Cadets wore their uniforms to class and in the evenings saluted officer upperclassmen at a soda joint called "The Coug," where the Stones and Buffalo Springfield played on the jukebox, and fifty years' worth of names were carved into the wooden booths.

Shawn Respert, who played for Michigan State, has said that Jud is a great shooting coach. Yes, I agree. Many times Jud walked over to me as I was warming up before practice and said, "Go ahead, shoot a couple." I would turn and shoot a jump shot from fifteen feet, and then another and another until he said, "OK, I see." Then he explained what I was doing and where I might change the shot—an adjustment here or there: hand on top of the ball, or elbow in and stop the ball. "This is a shot, not a throw," he would say. Or, "Turn and square up. Use your legs. Follow through." I remember how easily he seemed to analyze what I was doing, spot my problems in rhythm and form, and offer up a solution. A prosodist of the jump shot, he explained what I might look for—how the ball should spin slowly backward, how it should die on the rim when it hits, how a good shot hesitates in the net, falls through, hits the floor, and bounces back to you. "Ready, shoot" is the drill we would run and run. He passed the ball, and I caught it and set up in a shooting position, right hand behind and up on the ball, left hand supporting, elbow in, eyes on the basket, wait, wait, wait . . . "Shoot," he called, never quite when I expected it—shot opportunities and choices never the same twice, the theory goes—but the setup, the shot, the rhythm, the follow-through, these stay the same, practiced over and over until shooting is second nature.

Although his patience was suspect, Jud's motives never seemed in doubt. He wanted to win and he wanted us to be better basketball players. The outcome of the game mattered to him, but the more I played for Jud, the more I realized that how we reached that outcome mattered just as much. "Do what you can do. Leave the free-lancing at home! Where in hell did that come from? That's not your shot! Play the game we practiced." Each season I understood more how playing well meant balancing control and enthusiasm, how the discipline in practice showed in the games, and how focus during the game was a learned skill. If we were asleep on the floor, Jud provided a wake-up. Ironically, it's as if his strategy was meant to drive his players away from him and completely into the moment. The choice was either total concentration on the game or a bench-side critique with Jud.

Many factors provide tension in a game—the crowd, the opposing team, the fear of losing—but Jud provided the means, the reason, and the urgency. He was conductor, expert guide, ally, and scold. An event both of character and outcome, each game meant more to him than we could imagine. A national champion handball player who coached high school basketball as vigorously as college, who arranged his married life around a basketball schedule, who never in my recollection missed a practice or a game, this was a man whose life was competition. "Why don't you hang around the gym more?" he asked me one day. I didn't understand then what he was asking. The gym was where he lived. And it wasn't until in the locker room after one home game against California, when he called me a "hot dog" and an "embarrassment" for my mouthing off to the officials, for kicking the ball away, and for my self-righteous prima-donna antics, that I realized what Jud meant by playing well. It didn't seem to matter that their center, Bob Presley, kept barking in my ear that he was going to kick my honky mother-fuckin' ass, or that I scored over thirty points. We won the game, but I had lost something in Jud's eyes. When I was back in my own room with the door locked, alone and fighting back tears, I realized how painful it was not to be in Jud's good graces. He was a father, I think now, or perhaps my very own Orwellian headmaster, "goading, threatening, exhorting, sometimes joking, very occasionally praising, but always prodding away at one's mind to keep it up to the right pitch of concentration, as one might keep a sleepy person awake by sticking pins into him."

My antics that evening had earned Jud's worst criticism: "You're not *thinking.*"

There has always seemed to be a constructive tension between us. Even now. In one letter written a week or so before a 1992 Michigan State–Iowa game, he said, "Again we need all the help we can get in Iowa City; you have four tickets. We'll be staying at the Holiday Inn. Give me a call or drop by practice as we will be practicing 11:00–12:00 on February 6th. I look forward to seeing you. Maybe you can work on Pep's stick shot and the roll hook, or has memory and age dimmed your talents with both?" Sitting behind the Michigan State bench during warm-ups for that game, I tried to field a ball that had bounced off the floor, bobbled it slightly, and threw it back out to the players just as Jud walked up. "You could shoot but still can't catch," he said, shaking his head. I thought, *how typical.*

Ambiguity honed to an art form, his give-and-take language maintained a kind of suspension between reinforcement and criticism, between satisfaction and wanting more. He was pleased, yet hard to please. "So far so good," he seemed to be saying, "All right as far as it goes." I remember an awful shot I took once—too far out, a turnout, the stick shot that Jud despised but begrudgingly allowed by the time I was a junior for want of something better—a shot I had no business taking, having decided ahead of time I was due. I sailed back in my fadeaway, twenty feet out, and hoisted the ball toward the basket, the arc high as I heard from the bench, "No, no, what the hell . . . no business . . ." and "nice shot" as the ball fell through.

No one was immune. "You know better. You're the best jumper [shooter, defender, ball handler, etc.] on our team, so when are you going to play like it?" Such undercurrents. Such riptides. There were no opportunities to float on what he said. I remember his saying before a practice one day, "I want you to be a great basketball player, not just a good one." Was it praise or criticism? I still wonder. When I heard Stanley Kunitz say once that he didn't worry about all the bad poems being written, only about the ones just good enough, I thought of Jud's high standards and pressure to meet them, his urgent and focused poetics of concentration, thought, rhythm, and movement.

It was inevitable, I guess, that such a dynamic tension might find its limits. Coaches and players define each other's roles—a player learns from the coach and plays for him, and the coach sees the results of his work through the performance of his player. Given the pressure and the application of power in such a relationship, the tolerances need to be clearly defined. Some players at Washington State had no tolerance whatsoever for Jud. Others never seemed bothered. When I was a freshman, for example, the seniors of the varsity—Dale Ford, Ted Werner, and a few other players who seemed far older, rougher, and wiser than I—listened more to Harshman and less to Jud, unfazed, it seemed, by his tirades. Green and heedless, I tried to stay out of each coach's line of fire. It was a strategy that worked until my junior year, when the falling-out came.

On the court, the first string was assigned to defend the "gray" squad in a half-court defense drill. The gray squad had been taught the opponent's offense, and we were supposed to stop them with our man-to-man defense. I was guarding Dave Kessler, an all-American high hurdler, who was six-foot-six and constructed entirely of elbows, knees, and angles. Obedient and enthusiastic, Kessler, who played the game at two speeds—fidget-in-place or full-ahead—had the dubious distinction on our team of having shot, during games, air balls on three successive layups, the most infamous of which hit the backboard and bounced twenty feet back onto the court. Though he lacked a delicate touch, he was extremely fast and eager to please, sporting, despite the sixties, a flattop which stood up on its own.

It was late in the practice. I was tired and needed to sit down. My job was to prevent Kessler, the mock center for the opposing team, from breaking from his low-post position across the key and establishing position on the other side. His movement was predicated on following the ball around the perimeter, forward to point guard to opposite forward. When the ball left the point guard's hand, Kessler was supposed to break. I was supposed to block him high or low, forcing him high toward the free throw line or low toward the out-of-bounds line under the basket. Then I had to front him to spoil the pass in from the forward. All this meant I had to have an idea where he was going and move quickly enough to get in his way.

Jud set the play up. Kessler bounced on his toes as if he were ready for the starting gun. I got into position, anticipating the break. Standing beneath the basket, Jud blew the whistle. The ball went from one forward to the point guard, who caught it, and Kessler was simply gone. I don't remember if he went right or left, but I spun around just in time to hear Jud's whistle, strident and prolonged. "There's no way, son, you're going to stop anybody, standing around flatfooted. Jesus, move your feet." He had taken two steps toward me and then turned back. "Again, please." Most of the team had wandered some, hands on their hips, looking at the floor or the empty stands, trying to stay out of the mix, but Kessler had stayed in position, ready to go. I was the first-string center, the big shot. I was supposed to make this play.

Back now. With the whistle, the ball went from forward to point guard, who passed; Kessler jack-stepped me left—I fell for it—and then bounced right, buzz cut, elbows, and knees zipping by in a blur. I didn't even have time to grab his jersey. Jud's whistle reached a new octave. Here he was, red-faced in front of me. I backed up. Jud followed, hands out, demanding, "What the hell are you doing? Are you going to get this right today?" Out of the side of my eye, I could see Kessler grinning. Everyone else found something else to look at. This was the dreaded inquisition, Jud's auto-da-fé, and I was the heretic, singled out and guilty of slow feet and fatigue and a timid heart.

My final mistake, a response to embarrassment and a bruised ego, was to cheat—Kessler having won the moment and being anxious, I could see, to win the next. "Let's get it right this time," Jud said, and blew the whistle. Forward to point guard, who passed just as Kessler tried to jack-step again; I met him with a forearm shiver just beneath his armpit and punched, driving up and out so his upper body stayed put while his feet kept going up. Horizontal before he landed with a "whump" on his back on the floor, Kessler never got to the other side of the key. Vindicated and stupid, I didn't help him up.

Jud erupted, his whistle boiling over in the middle of a face as red as I had ever seen. He shuffle-trotted out toward me, fists clenched and head down, bull-like. Embarrassed and frustrated before, now I was scared, backing up as he got to me. I don't remember what he said for the ringing in my ears. I do remember my peripheral vision closing down as if his anger had grabbed at my shirt. My mouth was open, but I couldn't breathe. And then, bang,

bang, he started with his index finger pounding on my chest, once, twice . . . "Don't you ever—"

At the third bang, I broke ranks.

The telling takes far longer than my blocking his right arm away with my left hand and stepping with my left foot toward him, cocking my right fist so I could deliver the punch with authority. "Keep your fucking hands off me," I said, quicker than the instant, a slur muddled by fear and anger. I was pushed into a corner and snapping. He took two quick steps back and dropped his whistle, and in that moment we both stood on intolerant ground, far beyond any diagram, watching each other.

Until Coach Harshman stepped in.

"Now, now," he said, as if we were boys in a schoolyard. "We have a game to get ready for." The pontiff had spoken. Harshman, the final authority, refocused our energies on the abstract and holy. Jud was pit boss and teacher, but it was Harshman's team.

Jud and I didn't talk for the rest of the practice. That evening and all the next day, I agonized over what had happened. Fairy tales have this as the defining moment. The final breaking away. Conflict leads to self-sufficiency and independence. Jack cuts the beanstalk down. A mythological son strikes down his father when they meet anonymously, face-to-face on the road. I had never been so defiant of nor as violent with an authority figure. I was immediately lonely. Should I quit the team, or was I already off? Independent for a day, I wanted back in the fold. But that seemed impossible.

The next day, in language as sweet as a good play, Jud fixed it. After the boundaries had been overstepped and the tolerances squeezed down to zero, the first thing he said to me was, "Mind if I throw you a few passes?" I heard him behind me as I warmed up early before practice, by myself, at a far-corner basket in Bohler Gym.

"Sure," I said, turning and bouncing the ball to him to get ready for the "ready, shoot" drill.

"That is," he said, "if you don't hit me in the mouth."

"No," I said, "as long as you don't pound me in the chest if I make a mistake."

"Sounds fair to me," was all he said.

I have learned over the years that I am not the only player to have threatened a swing at Jud. Rumor has it that one of Jud's West Valley High players connected with a right cross, and Jud's response after he got up from the floor was, "That's the most heart you've shown all day." It seems in character. That a player-coach relationship would break down and even turn violent is no surprise. Coaches, from high school to professional, pressure their players, set goals, and make demands. Players need a coach to convince them the pain they are going through is worthwhile. There is a fine line here between push and shove. When that line is obliterated, it is the coach's job to redraw it. That's what Jud did. He took charge, and we all moved on.

When I was a senior, Pete the equipment manager finally talked to me. After three years of machinations and trials and seventy-four games, I felt as if I had earned respect from the coaches and my teammates, and could watch at the far end of the court the new freshmen squirm and grimace under their first year with Jud. Despite such seniority, the pressure was always on, though the tolerances had been discovered and respected both ways, coach and player.

Perhaps what tempered Jud's maniacal intensity for the game was that he seemed capable of perspective, whether through humor, self-parody, or simply by looking the other way. *Sports Illustrated* explains that "Heathcote . . . has a warmth about him, an awkward, gruff-uncle charm. He is most comfortable when turning the needle inward, and unlike Knight, he is incapable of taking himself seriously." True, there are many examples of Jud's self-deprecating humor. "Sooner or later, the game makes fools of us all," he has been quoted as saying. "And I guess I'm living proof." And I remember his being able to poke fun at himself—the time on a road trip, for example, he backed the car over his own suitcases. For thirty miles no one dared speak until someone said from the back seat, "They were easier to get in the trunk." Even Jud had to laugh. Or the time we finally beat Oregon State at Corvallis in the season's next-to-last game and spent the night in downtown Portland at the Benson Hotel. Dick Vandervoort, the trainer, gave us each five dollars to get something to eat. Then we were on our own in downtown Portland late on a Saturday night. I don't know whose idea it was to spend our five bucks at the topless nightclub three blocks north of the Benson, but six of us, four of whom were starters, headed for the night life, dressed in our crimson blazers with the Cougar insignias. We might as well have been wearing overalls and straw hats, as obvious as we were spread out in the front row, our five dollars spent on the two-drink minimum, the glasses weeping on the miniature tables. In blue light and with fine timing before us on stage, Fatima of the Nile rotated her tassels in opposite directions.

We were near deep hypnosis when the door opened and in walked Dick Vandervoort, Coach Harshman, and Jud. They took pains not to trip over us as they walked back behind us into the dark. No one turned to look. As the tassels slowed and we froze, out the door filed Dick Vandervoort, Coach Harshman, and then Jud, who turned to us, one hand on the door, and said, "This isn't the place we thought it was." The next day was a 250-mile trip from Portland to Pullman—a long, silent car ride home.

It's simply not true, however, that Jud is "incapable of taking himself seriously." None of his players worked for Jud's sense of humor. To see the look on his face when the Spartans won the national championship in 1979, or his despair in 1990 when Georgia Tech's Kenny Anderson tied the game on an unwhistled, after-the-buzzer shot, a game Georgia Tech then won in overtime, is to see a coach for whom the game means everything. Lear couldn't have looked more tragic. Basketball was always first. Opinions, one-liners, wit, green blazers, and a bad hairstyle notwithstanding, the forty minutes on the court is serious business indeed.

Watching Michigan State practice on one of their visits to Iowa City, I realized that Jud's teams have always been a reflection of his character—serious, playful, and urgent. There was Jud on the floor at the end of practice, trying to face guard Shawn Respert, who moved left and right and called for the ball. "Mismatch, mismatch," Respert yelled, laughing. How true, both ways. Jud was sixty-four with a bad knee, but Respert played Jud's game.

So did we all. I would like to think I took from my four years a sense of form and rhythm, of creative tension, the ability to concentrate, the need to get things right, and a friendship that has lasted years beyond my eligibility. In 1986 when *Headlong,* my first book of poems, was published, I sent a copy to Jud. He wrote back, "Thanks so much for your book of poems. This is the first of many you will be famous for some day and I will be able to say 'I knew him when.' I do hope sooner or later you will be able to figure out one that rhymes. Remember, you can always start, 'Roses are red, Violets are Blue' and go from there. I do plan to study them all and maybe sooner or later it will make me a smarter basketball coach." He ended his letter by saying, "I am looking forward to seeing you February 6. Count on four tickets as usual as we need all the support we can get."

I wrote back to thank him for the tickets and to say I wasn't sure if my poems would make him a smarter basketball coach, but I knew playing basketball for him had certainly made me a better poet. My legs are gone, but my memory hasn't dimmed. Michigan State won by a point that evening on a three-point shot at the buzzer, picked up their water bottles and towels, and escaped to East Lansing before the Iowa crowd had a chance to sit back down. As the gym emptied out, I sat and waited, thinking of my divided loyalties. An Iowa alum now, I live in Iowa City and follow the Hawkeye basketball team, but here I was sitting all evening in a row of green sweaters, rooting for Michigan State. No, I was rooting for Jud. Ever since I left Washington State University, left home in effect, I have been loyal to Marv Harshman and Jud. They helped me grow up. And even though I don't play basketball much anymore, preferring the humility of tennis after a day of words, I still hear their voices. They have left me something parental, a kind of conscience that speaks from courtside, saying in reference to whatever I do or make, "Too much here or not enough there," or "Effort, please, effort," or "Terrific"—followed always by "try again."

D/ALTERED

THE RED LIGHT MEANS YOU'RE READY TO GO. IT'S ON TOP OF THE starter's Christmas tree. Ominous and ironic. In this world, red means you're staged, your front wheels having entered the timing lights. If you ask what drove you here or if you'll drive away, consider it a bad joke. On second thought, maybe it's a good question. How did you get into this—strapped in and petrified? Think about it. You're straddling three hundred cubic inches of six-cylinder in-line Hudson Hornet engine and its two-speed dynaflow transmission bolted to a chrome-moly-tubing, heliarc-welded, shortened-slingshot dragster frame with a fiberglass roadster body. If you're knocking your helmet-encased head against the Kandi blue metal-flake roll bar, it's because the lights on the Christmas tree have fallen to yellow, you've got the engine revved to stall speed against the brakes, and in the pits and on the sidelines Steve Henshaw and all your dubious partners expect you to smoke the slicks the whole quarter mile in your very own handcrafted, scavenged, and jury-rigged D/Altered dragster.

The Puyallup Raceway in the summer of 1965. I'm nineteen. I should be shooting baskets at the "Y." Instead I've shoveled half my asphalt laborer's summer wages into a machine the purpose of which is simply hormonal—all adrenalin and acceleration, all held breath and grunting and explosion, all noise and smoking tires. It's fireworks you can ride. It's impatient and absolutely self-centered sex, the point of which is to get it over with as quickly and with as much enthusiasm as possible. It's testosterone renamed alcohol, or high-test injected, or nitromethane supercharged and blown so that ten-foot acetylene hot flames rocket from those slingshot top-fuelers, four out each zoomie header like brilliant white-blue diabolic candelabras. Cover your ears, it hurts that much. Even fifty feet away, the sound whaps your body like a broom against a carpet.

Another yellow. Admit it. Come on. Think. It's more than a twelve-second ride. It's more than my weight tripled in Gs, or the redundant maniac with his starter's flag down on his knees, ready to swat flies. I don't need his OK. Fess up. There's something to love in the language of all this, though I would never tell my crew that—Henshaw up to his elbows in oil, knuckles busted, or Billy with his grinding tools, near tears at the prospect of dismantling the largest six-cylinder flathead cast after World War II, the 1953 Hudson Hornet 5,047 cc behemoth Henshaw found in a junkyard and convinced me to haul in my father's Ford station wagon—its leaf springs were never the same—back to Billy's shop so he could stroke and bore and port and polish. The assonance and alliteration sold me, as if the engine would breathe again, as if the very words themselves greased the bearings.

Or how the holy catalogs turned my head, their gospel the text I pored over column after column. Salvation lay somewhere in the Moon Equipment Company inventory, its stock of manifolds and magnetos. And Honest Charley, the graffiti man and car-parts huckster "hisself," pointing in his ads like Uncle Sam or Elmer Gantry, freed you from the conventions of grammar in his "Honest

Price Catalog." As long as I kept turning the page, a litany of names and parts echoed in my ears like a roll call of saints: Iskenderian the cam grinder, Mallory and his magnetos, Edelbrock of the manifold, Jahns forged pistons, Hurst of the spring-loaded four-on-the-floor, Hedman Hedders, Halibrand of the rear end and mag wheels, Hilborn the fuel injector. Offenhauser and Eelco, Grant rings and Getz gears. Traction Master and Cal Custom. Oh, how they moved me, those names all sibilance and repetition, a revving of consonants and chrome. Headlong, full speed, bustin' loose, the euphony wound me clear to imagination's red line.

And it cost nothing to say these names as if speaking would qualify me to stand before drag racing's pantheon, a kind of incantatory pit pass so that I might enter into the presence of "Big Daddy" Don Garlits and Don "The Snake" Prudhomme and Rick "The Iceman" Stewart, drivers so fast only their nicknames kept up. Mickey Thompson, Brooks and Rapp, the Northwest's own Jerry Ruth, the Baromas brothers, Danny Ongais, the Sandoval brothers, and Mooneyham, Ferguson, Jackson, and Faust. Said all at once, they sound like latter-day gunslingers who listen to rock 'n' roll and make pacts with the nitro devil.

Piece by piece our D/Altered cost plenty. Woops. Another yellow light for the heart. We painted "Henshaw and McKean" on the back of our catalog-special, Acme Freight–delivered model "A" ersatz-fiberglass coupe body, because we wanted to drive our names as fast as we could into hot-rod recognition. We asked Tacoma's Thane Porlier to build the frame. Who else? Sculptor Thane. An artist in chrome-moly. Baron Thane. Thane of Cawdor. Holder of the welding torch. Who sat me on his workbench to measure me butt to brow for the enormous roll bar. The frame all steel tubing and heliarc welds, the junkyard Olds rear end and axle chopped and narrowed, as if this car were a tailored suit of armor.

Thane cut and welded the steel headers. He built the axles and radius rods and kingpins, and set the spindles and caster, and bolted in the drag link and steering box.

The steering wheel we lifted from Billy's go-cart. We ordered a two-gallon polished-aluminum gas tank from Moon Auto, round chrome filter caps to sparkle atop the dual single-choke "Twin-H Power" Hudson carburetors, a pair of steel rims to fit the used ten-inch slicks Henshaw found at a hot rodder's yard sale, and a new aluminum head and gaskets for the Hudson Billy had ported and polished to perfection. A new cam, valves, plugs, metal-flake paint job, junkyard front rims, and on-sale six-dollar black-walled tires. Fasteners and tubes and fittings and firewalls. Scavenge and search and toil and trouble.

Yellow. There's someone in the lane next to me, but I haven't got the nerve to look. Too late to turn my head, all bound up sitting in my purloined plastic lawn chair bolted to the frame and held by shoulder straps and seat belts over my borrowed aluminum and asbestos-lined safety jacket, my helmet full of sweat, the visor fogged, the Hudson six spasmodic, epileptic, groaning against the brakes, the brake lever tight in my right hand, my left on the wheel. Hold it. Hold it. Too late to add a Moon foot-shaped gas pedal. Too late to add spoke wheels. Too late and no money to add a magneto—a Rube Goldberg Ray-o-Vac tied-to-the-Hudson-with-hemp-rope ignition system standing in, a spark from the profane for the finely tuned and chrome-plated sublime . . .

Green. Oh, god. Brake off. Foot down. Hands on the wheel. The Hudson sucks the air blue, growling like a diesel, the whole D/Altered hunching as if jabbed in the rear, smoke billowing from the tires, my head popped back, helmet clanking against the roll bar. Whining. Point it straight. Higher. The RPMs vibrating my teeth, the crowd left behind, the track before me all vanishing point, trees a green blur. Wait, wait. Shift once. Left hand down. Right on the wheel. The dynaflow thumps into drive and the big six settles into its shoulders and back muscles and growls and stuffs me into the seat, wind filling my collar and flattening the face shield, the finish line, the timing booth, the black-and-white finish banner growing larger faster, faster and faster. Heart thumping, mouth open, I think I'm a driver, that I will make one small steering adjustment, the car drifting, the run still accelerating, just a little turn on the wheel back toward the middle of my lane, and clank.

Then nothing.

How suddenly the world goes metaphoric. How curious and calm such moments seem. My first thought is sentimental—the little red car on its pedestal outside the Safeway store. How my mother stood next to me and plugged dimes into the slot so the car rocked back and forth and I could steer frantically nowhere—I knew even then—the wheel turning round and round and round. And then I remember the awful wreck of the Baromas brothers' supercharged hemi Anglia, so overpowered and souped up it looked like an Ed Roth "Rat Fink" hyperbolic cartoon; how the driver goosed the car sideways, let off, goosed it again twice as hard, and the car leaped straight up, pitched onto its nose, and dove into the asphalt, disintegrating halfway up the track right in front of me. Remember the ambulances and red lights, the engine broken loose, upside down and leaking its oil, the driver lying next to it, moaning, his helmet ripped off, still alive though his right leg bent under him four different ways. Oh, man, Jim, think about this—your steering is gone.

Next week, Thane Porlier will admit that he should have sleeved the rod connecting the steering box and the lever gears. That butt weld just couldn't stand the torque. But I don't know this yet. All I know is that the wheel spins free. All I see is the finish line here and gone. All they see in the booth is a D/Altered flashing by, its crazy driver with both hands on the brake lever bending it by his right ear, the engine sighing and backfiring and decompressing.

No one seems worried, although Henshaw and Billy in the tow car had to search to find me, having rolled far past the finish area down a dirt road and into the pine woods, both of my hands still yanking on the brake. But I have a new understanding. Shut off, the engine steams and tinks, heat waffling the air. Henshaw unbuckles me and slaps my shoulder for the time and speed. "Twelve point nine," he says. "Terrific. And 124 miles per hour."

"Well, I didn't have a hand in it," I say, but no one gets it. My knees wobble the rest of the day. My thinking wobbles a lot longer than that.

When Thane asks what's the worry, and says, "Hey, we designed it to go straight," and explains the physics behind fifteen-degree axle tilt and kingpins and the gyroscope effect and wheel flop, all I hear are the puns. I need to think about this and beg off drag racing the next few weeks. Then I beg off for good, playing basketball instead three nights a week at the "Y" and lifting weights, my sophomore season at Washington State University only months away. I reread poems from my English classes, the language now more poignant than ever. Grasping the obvious, I discover words really mean something. Roethke says, "I learn by going where I have to go," and Stafford negotiates the dark, his exhaust red. Words such as "headlong," "steering," "acceleration," "full speed," "brakes," and "deep woods" spark and roll and rumble.

And when I rediscover Robert Creeley's poem "I Know a Man," the summer compresses itself into his lines:

> *. . . the darkness sur-*
>
> *rounds us, what*

can we do against
it, or else, shall we &
why not, buy a goddamn big car,

drive, he sd, for
christ's sake, look
out where yr going.

I copy the poem and carry it in my wallet, admonished by word and circumstances—and my father, who mentions my dangerous quarter mile in passing, eyebrow raised, just once.

It is 1965. I try to look where I'm going in an impetuous time that seems to be accelerating way too fast. Music. Riots. Vietnam. I go to school. I play ball. I read and love words and try to write poems with speed and rhythm. There are language wrecks galore, but each is survivable. And when I look over my shoulder, it's to be thankful again I made it through my wild run—twenty-odd seconds with no steering—and to see what kind of times Henshaw and Billy are posting, to write them letters, and then to wonder what they will do after the Hudson throws a rod and Henshaw gets drafted and Billy joins up. And months later, to hope they make it back from their over-revved, fully blown, and flat-out tours in Vietnam—Steve Henshaw, race-car driver and welder, who does, and Billy—I hear one day—sweet Billy, artist of the port and polish, who doesn't.

LEARNING TO FIGHT

FIVE PARAGRAPHS INTO RICHARD FORD'S *NEW YORKER* ESSAY "IN the Face," I realized it had taken me years to recognize such men, and even longer to stay the hell away from them. Analyzing his own penchant for confrontation and physical violence, Ford explains how he grew up in the fifties in Mississippi and Arkansas, where hitting someone in the face "meant something." It meant you were brave, experienced, impulsive, dangerous, and moving toward "adulthood, the place we were all headed—a step in the right direction." *Oh no,* I thought, *here we go again.* By the end of the essay, where he says that he himself is a man "who could be willing to hit you in the face" in response to "some enmity, some affront, some inequity or malfeasance," I wanted to find an Exit sign.

The trouble is, I understand his essay all too well, having experienced both sides of these mix-ups. I too grew up in the fifties—and kept growing beyond reason—a tall, skinny kid trying to survive in a landscape full of junked cars and gravel driveways. By the time I was a senior in high school, I stood two inches shy of seven feet. An odd duck, adrift above a sea of heads, I was either invisible or the target for incredulity, jokes, insults, challenges, threats, and a variety of punches. When such a difference in size appeared as an "inequity" or an "affront," to repeat Richard Ford's triggers, it often invited reprisal.

On the other hand, as a boy trying to survive in a tough neighborhood, who learned where to hide and what escape routes led deep into the woods, who suffered the bloody nose and cut lip of beatings time and again, who dished it out, who took it, who gave unto and received thereof, I must admit that I committed my share of assaults—even on the basketball court, my salvation and retreat, where violence should be metaphoric and under control. For this I would like to offer an explanation, an apologia of sorts.

There is one wrong-headed mix-up in the past that I replay over and over. Thirty-five years ago, I feared my Washington State basketball team was about to lose to Oregon State. My parents sat six rows up behind our team bench, having driven three hundred miles from Tacoma, Washington, to watch us play against the Beavers at Slats Gill Coliseum in Corvallis. With twenty seconds to go in the game, we were losing by one point. Oregon State had the ball out of bounds, and we hustled back into a full-court press, the din awful and metallic. I was the Cougar's center, the back defensive man.

All orange and black, Oregon State wore crew cuts and high-top tennis shoes. Too confident to begin with, I was now frantic in this dimly lit cavern of a gym with its ridiculous, bucktoothed mascot gnawing on the grandstand. The crowd's roar squeezed my chest. My ears rang. Maybe my pride suffered and I wanted someone to pay. I saw Loy Peterson, Oregon State's cocky, six-foot-five star forward—a wise guy, an arrogant trash-talker—loping up the floor, all nonchalance. I saw the inbounds pass, an overhand throw in slow motion arcing up and then down toward Peterson as he crossed the ten-second line. I saw the intersection, the point where

Peterson and the ball would meet. I took off sprinting from our free-throw line, hoping to get there first. As Peterson looked over his shoulder and lifted his arms, I left my feet at full speed.

° ° °

LIKE LIFE, BASKETBALL IS A GAME OF CONTROL, A GAME OF MIS-takes. During pregame pep talks, our coaches always explained that the team that made the fewest mistakes would win. "Play within yourself," they would counsel. "Give your energy to the game. Discipline. Concentration."

Like anyone trying to grow up, I had been working on those skills for a long time—at least since an ignominious dustup in the seventh grade, when I tried to lay out Gary Huffer with a punch worthy of John Wayne in *The Quiet Man.* Quick-witted and baiting, my dubious friend picked at me all afternoon about my clothes, my haircut, my forgetfulness—it didn't matter—until I flailed at him and connected a glancing blow on his teeth. All my patty-cake did was enrage Gary, and he lunged at me. We fell to wrestling. If I hold my fist up in front of my nose, I can still see the faint scar, a small shiny crescent more than forty years old, and remember the blood running down my hand and my feeling misunderstood and pitiful.

Maybe seven years later and a foot taller, I wondered if the jerk standing on the sidewalk outside a South Tacoma dance hall, the blood running down his fingers and dropping onto the sidewalk, felt pitiful. This time my teeth had cut his knuckle. "Hey, man, I don't take no shit from nobody," he told the cop who had walked me out of the dance hall with my arm hammerlocked behind my back. Obviously the cop assumed I had started this. Don't all big guys start trouble? When I bent down to show him the gap in my teeth, and my assailant took the cigarette from his mouth with his blood-covered right hand, the cop figured it out.

"What did you think you were doing? Take a look," the cop said to the guy, pointing at me.

"Man, he was swearing at me. I was in Vietnam, man," he said plaintively, as if that were reason enough for striking out.

"So? This guy's big enough to beat the shit out of two of you. You want that? Get lost," the cop said.

What the vet wanted was justice or simply a beating, his or mine. Maybe the cop didn't care about the former and assumed I knew how to execute the latter. Having been sucker-punched while sitting in a dance hall minding my own business, I preferred a little justice. Now I faced a lifetime of root canals and porcelain caps.

But the cop fell back on the old cliché—if you look big enough to intimidate, to stand there emblematic of Richard Ford's "inequity," your head and shoulders blocking out the streetlight, well, shouldn't you be able to wreak havoc, mow them down, take care of business? It didn't matter to him that a stranger had walked up to my table, leaned on my shoulder and said, "You're not so big," and patted me openpalmed on the cheek.

"Get away from me, asshole," I said. His open hand turned into a fist and smashed hard into my mouth. I heard a thud and click, and stood up, the lower half of my mouth numb. With my tongue I could feel my left front tooth pointing toward the back of my mouth. The tooth next to it, my left incisor, was gone altogether. The son of a bitch had hit me. Now he stood two steps back, whining and making his case.

"You swore at me, man. I don't take that from no one."

° ° °

I SHOULD HAVE SEEN IT COMING. THEN I MIGHT HAVE BEEN ABLE to do something about it. Growing up, I fantasized about defending myself in just such situations. I studied the Charles Atlas ads at the back of *Superman* comic books. Certain that I was the ninety-eight-pound weakling with sand kicked in my face, I wrote to the address for my salvation. I wanted to be the comeback hero, my fist a lightning bolt like the Charles Atlas graduate in the final cartoon panel, the bully stunned at last to his knees. I suspected the girl hanging on the hero's arm had something to do with all this, but at that time in my life, I thought a good right cross more useful.

My childhood nemesis, Mickey Scott, strutted and steamed every day in his front yard across the street. At the bus stop each morning, all the Vitalis-haired, sleeve-rolled, low-pants, cigarette-smoking eighth-graders loitered, each one a threat. A pack mentality ruled. Fear dictated where you walked and when, and made every antagonist huge. Then, at the park after school, there was Stevie Yates, his grunting big brother always within earshot, giving me the finger. He did the same thing one morning to our part-time music teacher, a sullen, skinny man with curly black hair, who proceeded in great conductorial sweeps to rip Stevie Yates's shirt off. Someone must have called Stevie's mother, for she marched squint-eyed into the middle of our sixth-grade class just before lunch, muttering "Never again," and hauled Stevie out of his chair by the naked arm and dragged him out the door, the still-buttoned collar of his shirt like a horseshoe ringing his neck.

Charles Atlas sent me a catalog and an order form for weights and food supplements, available by check, money order, or COD. I had none of the above. I duct-taped bricks to two-by-fours. That summer, when my neighbor was pouring concrete for his driveway, I persuaded him to fill two coffee cans, which I then stuck on the ends of a piece of pipe. I lifted and lifted. A week later I was still skinny. I took judo in gym class and learned how to fall down. I watched *The Lone Ranger* and *The Cisco Kid* and the *Friday Night Fights* with my dad, who idolized Rocky Marciano and Joe Louis. Then, in the eighth grade, I tried out for the school basketball team because I could shoot the ball like Bob Petit at my backyard basket.

The junior high coach, Jack Johnson, cut me two days later. Brokenhearted, I tried out for a local Optimist Club team that needed one more player. Then two things happened that cemented basketball as my raison d'être: I grew five inches in six months, and I saw my name in the paper. A little ink and my life turned round. "Jim McKean scored the winning field goal in overtime to give the SEJO Pirates a 16-15 decision over St. Patrick's in a bantam League boys' basketball thriller yesterday." A one-inch filler under the local sports news buried somewhere on page 50 of the *Tacoma News Tribune* read for me like neon lights in a picture window. Jack Johnson saw the light the next year when I was in ninth grade, started me at center, and I played for years and years after that.

° ° °

What I never developed was a lightning-bolt right hand. Growing straight up, I had too much else to learn. I remember being sixteen, carefree for a moment in the summer, listening to "Duke of Earl" as I strode through my mother's kitchen, heedless and head bobbing, only to crack my forehead on the top of the dining room door. The house shook. My eyes crossed. Ears ringing and lights popping, I had discovered the edge of the world at last. The standard world, that is, for all manufactured things are measured to a norm. As I kept growing, the world stuck out its knees and elbows. Nothing fit. Not clothes, not cars, not the desks at school. All the graphs and tables for measuring height and weight stopped before I stopped. When I sat down in a movie theater, the people behind me groaned and moved five seats over. Once when a friend let me drive his MG Midget sports car, I wedged myself in but got my feet stuck behind the pedals, the car whining in second gear as I four-wheel-drifted around the corners of his neighborhood until I saw him again waving frantically, turned the key off, and rolled to a stop so he could pry me out.

No sleeping bags or backpacks. No spelunking. No basements. No cabin cruisers. No airplane seats. No slow-dancing cheek to cheek. No calm and carefree moments while navigating the world, for there were lamps and tables and chairs and glassware balanced everywhere—a panorama of traps. My reach far exceeded my grasp, and bless the poor wreckage in between. All my pants needed letting down. My shirttail hung free. In the back room, the Bon Marché found me one pair of shoes, in brown. Chandeliers, no. Beds, only partway, and please, no footboards. The Navy? Forget it. The Army? I wasn't regulation. No hauling. No wheelbarrows. No rakes, no lawn mowers, no short-handled shovels. No drinking fountains or bathroom mirrors. My back hurt from stooping, and when I stood up, there were always those infernally adamant doors. Symbol and fact. The building-code standard door is six foot eight inches high. By the time I was a senior in high school, I could rest my eyebrows on the top edge of the doorframe. Duck or else. The choice was simple.

In a world where objects and attitudes conform to a standard, ducking seemed wise. But such conditioning took time and attention. "Watch where you're going," my father said, as most fathers do, though I realized quickly he meant in front of my nose as well as long-range. The world is an obstacle course, before and behind, above and below. Watch where you put your feet. Watch your head. And I did, the learning curve sharp and painful. Soon ducking became second nature. I began to grow accustomed to tight spaces, as if I could sense intuitively where the edges were, and how far I could reach, and where all the corners cut into whatever journey I was on. Basketball helped, of course. And although I never developed a good right cross, I did learn one important boxing skill—I could slip the world's punches. Doors weren't going to give, so I did, reflexively, just enough to miss, nodding as I passed through to the simple and unchangeable fate of it all.

Attitudes, however, prove far more problematic. In his essay "The Body and the Earth," Wendell Berry explains that in our culture, "the appropriate standard for the body—that is, health—has been replaced . . . by very exclusive physical models, a narrowly defined ideal which affects destructively whatever it does not include." Boys should be "tall," Berry says, "but not too tall." I have discovered that standing so much larger than these "models" excludes me, at times, from standard courtesies as well, as if social boundaries apply only to those falling within the range of the physically normal. Otherwise, anything goes. Laughter, pointing, gawking, open-mouthed incredulity followed by a litany of inane questions concerning my heritage, the weather up there, clothing, marital relationships and the physical possibilities thereof. The most worrisome attitude I face from others is fear and hostility, which all too quickly translate into indignation that I appear to occupy more than my fair share of the earth's surface, or that I am a king of the mountain who needs to be deposed.

"This too will pass," I have said to myself at such times, and there is some comfort in Blake's proverb, "He who has suffered you to impose on him knows you." The problem is what to do with such knowledge once you have it. The most visceral and least acceptable response is confrontation. Maybe that is why Richard Ford's essay rings so true for me. Embarrassed more often than I can remember, threatened, frightened, sad, and defensive, I have wanted to strike back, the impulse primitive and reptilian. With power and skill—quick wits and even quicker fists—I have wanted to get my due, deliver the comeuppance, and even the score. Charles Atlas knew the situation. Every Saturday-matinee cowboy I admired packed a quick-fix right hand. And all the neighborhood tough guys of my growing up—Chic Frisell, Squire Tomassi, Dean Lloyd, Jim Allotta—they knew what to say and how to back it up.

° ° °

BY THE TIME I WAS PLAYING BASKETBALL IN COLLEGE, I HAD fashioned a terrific fadeaway jump shot—but even that was useless in a dustup. Barn-toppling haymakers remained academic. Watching the fights on TV with my father, I cheered Floyd Patterson's revenge knockout of Ingmar Johanson. I applauded Muhammad Ali's phantom punch, as the bully Liston, all imposition and bluff, lay faceup on the canvas. I loved the anticipation and then the boxing event itself, and the language of the body and force—right cross, left hook, jab and uppercut, dodge, parry, slip and counter. I longed to know how such words were put into practice, how the mind and the fist work as one, and I pestered the few boxers I knew to explain.

"It's all hand and foot speed," explained my friend and classmate Terry Davis, who had fought in the Golden Gloves and wanted to be a writer like Jack London. I listened, fascinated by his stories and envious of his skill. A street fighter by reputation in his hometown of Richland, Terry always excused himself before a fight, rumor had it, to go home and find his mouthpiece. Then he returned.

"I'll fight you, but not any of your buddies over there," he would say, pointing with the mouthpiece he held in his left hand at whoever stood at some distance out of range. Woe to the tough guy who let his eyes follow that left hand, for the moment he turned his head, his jaw lifting ever so slightly, Terry nailed him with a short straight right—aiming for the wisdom teeth, I assume. That usually ended it, Terry said.

"But what if someone really knows how to fight?" I asked.

"Well, no one takes their eyes off you in the Golden Gloves, so you have to watch and plan. I fought the Idaho champion in Lewiston once. Strong kid. He threw everything at me the first two rounds. I could only jab and cover, but he got tired. Started announcing his right. He'd step with his left foot, wind up that big right hand, and then drop his head more and more as he threw the punch. Any pattern's a mistake. Thirty seconds into the third round, he stepped with his left foot, started the right, and I aimed my uppercut at a place I thought his head would be. Sure enough. Down it came. I really twisted into that punch. Felt it in my back, my hips—you know, solid."

"What about someone like me? A foot taller? Heavier?"

"You'd be easy," Terry said. I took a little umbrage until he showed me. He stood me in position, fists up, and then suddenly I couldn't get rid of Terry Davis. Under my arms, his forehead on my chest, left leg stepping through my feet, he turned me toward my right so I was off balance, my hands grabbing at the air behind him. As if in reflex, I kept pulling my left elbow back down to get rid of the annoying *tap tap* in my ribs, while he pushed me back on my heels around the room in a circle. "See, see?" he said, from somewhere inside my shirt, "I'd be here the whole time."

In her book *On Boxing,* Joyce Carol Oates explains that for some people fighting activates an "adrenalin rush" as well as an "atavistic self," angry and predatory. Something in Terry's demeanor—meanness and the joy to act on it—frightened the hell out of me. But he was smart and disciplined and willing to subordinate his aggression to technique and skill. He learned to be a good boxer.

The master of such skill at Washington State University was Ike

Deeter, the boxing coach. The word was that any ambitious tough guy on campus had to serve time with Deeter, preferably enrolled in his boxing class. One of my roommates signed up, brought home two pairs of sixteen-ounce boxing gloves, and three days a week sported the red outline of Ace headgear on his face. Mark talked incessantly about Ike Deeter: Deeter didn't talk much at all. Showed you. Old guy but he could hurt you bad, beat your arms numb until you couldn't hold them up. Famous for his one-inch punch demonstration on some unlucky freshman the first day of class. All body, short straight line, and follow-through, and that made all the difference.

I have since read that Ike Deeter fought as a 160-pounder when he was in high school in Spokane, Washington. A Golden Gloves champion in 1927 and 1928, he was recruited to play football for Washington State University, but suffered a knee injury and went back to boxing. After graduating in 1929, he was hired to coach the Washington State University boxing team, which he did until Washington State dropped boxing as an intercollegiate sport in 1959. After that, Ike Deeter taught his boxing class somewhere in Bohler Gym. During basketball practice sometimes, I could hear the tattoo of a light bag or the *tack tack tack* of someone jumping rope.

Once as I bent over the drinking fountain in the hallway outside the basketball court, exhausted and sweat soaked after three hours of practice, a gray-haired man shuffled toward me and stopped a moment as I stood up. He didn't look directly at me or away. He seemed to see all of me at once—where I held my hands and how I turned my body and just how far apart we were. I knew right away this was Ike Deeter. About five foot eight and probably still 160, he wore gray pants and a gray T-shirt marked "Property of WSU Athletics." As square as his name, his face looked roughed up and healed, what you would expect of a boxer and a football player who had never used a facemask. He held his hands easy and a little bit away from his sides. Intimidated for some reason and cautious, I took a step back and said, "Hi, Coach." He nodded and sidestepped me and kept on down the hallway.

That evening, I told my roommate I had run into his inimitable boxing coach. Tossing me a pair of gloves, Mark said, "Here, try these on and I'll show you Deeter's lesson for the day."

"I don't know . . ." I said, trying to beg off.

"You're a big guy. A helluva lot bigger than me. What's the problem? We'll just spar. You got all the advantage."

I should have known better. Five minutes later, I tried to unlace the boxing gloves with my teeth, the bells still pealing in my head. Although I never saw the punch, I should have recognized how my chum set me up. *Don't rise to the bait,* I keep telling myself, *because it will never end.* I am thinking of Richard Ford's knee-jerk response to "inequity" again, how my simply walking up to him might strike some reptilian chord, some visceral need to wipe out difference, and he would "hit me in the face."

° ° °

MAYBE. MAYBE NOT. BUT IT PAYS TO PAY ATTENTION. IF KNUCKles are the least sophisticated option, it also pays to invent alternate coping strategies in a world quick to regard difference as odd, alien, and a threat. That is, unless you would like to mix it up every day.

One economical and face-saving strategy is retreat. I remember walking into the Roundup Bar and Grill one night in Kennewick, Washington—"Hoedown Every Friday," the sign said—and waiting for my eyes to adjust. The first thing into focus was a white, snap-button shirt—one sleeve rolled, the other unrolled and flapping—and then the cowboy wearing it, no hat anywhere. His face seemed flushed and a little puffy. Maybe he had been dancing, for his hair lay matted against his forehead. On his table sat two empty shot glasses next to tall Buds and a pack of Camels, the ashtray full, one cigarette still lit, an empty chair across from him. He was about thirty.

The moment he caught sight of me, I knew he itched to make my acquaintance. A menace or a curiosity, or simply someone whose height seemed strange to him, out of his ken and therefore a threat, maybe I represented the wilderness, the unknown. I don't know. I wasn't in the mood to find out. The cowboy pushed his chair back with one hand, the other hand on the table, which tilted, bottles clanking over. Stumbling, no doubt angry at that already, he squinted at me as he rose and said, "Hey, you."

Bye-bye, I thought, and turned quickly, not having stood in the dark a minute, and headed toward the Exit sign. I remember finding on the sidewalk blood that hadn't been there when I went in, an emblem of the Roundup, certainly. Retreat had guaranteed that none of it would be mine.

Another strategy is the clown or Step 'n' Fetchit routine, especially if retreat isn't an option and survival is at stake. Forget about boundaries, especially your own. Imagine yourself riding a 750 four-cylinder Honda motorcycle from Pullman and descending from the Paloose wheat hills into Washtucna, a farm community halfway between Pullman and your home in Pasco, Washington. It is September and shivering cold in the hollows. You need gas and time to thaw out your core. Here is the Washtucna Tavern beside two locked gas pumps. You park and lean the bike on its stand. You straighten your knees and back, take your helmet off, turn the doorknob, and duck into smoke.

Not everything stops. The pinball player still chucks and slaps at his machine. The jukebox plays something country, Tammy Wynette or the Oak Ridge Boys. But conversation dies. A gallery of seed caps rises up as your eyes adjust. Someone says, "Whoa." If you sit down quickly, you might sneak in, a momentary head and shoulders in the haze, but someone steps in your way before you get to the empty bar stool.

"Grow 'em big where you come from," the man in overalls says. He peers at you as his wife steps up and says, "My oh my, look at those pant legs," and tugs at the denim so your cuff rides up, probably to see if it is really you in there.

"Thought you were standing on something when you walked in," the man says. Three more hats gather round, tipped back with the long necks of beer bottles.

"Nope. Just my feet," you say, making sure to smile and nod and even shuffle some, one foot to the other. It is self-deprecating and calming somehow, a kind of physical "Aw, shucks." Answer questions about your parents, basketball, the weather, the doorways, shoes, clothing, your knees in cars and motorcycles. But if one of the young men lifts his girlfriend onto a chair so she is looking you straight in the eye—she'll be pretty and red-faced and embarrassed to be there—don't kiss her. "Tough to dance on a chair," you might say, and "Folks in Washtucna sure have a good time," and "I sure could use a bowl of soup." By now, you have been bagged and tagged. Interest wanes. The beers are empty. The pinball machine still dings and whistles. The song on the jukebox is all about loss. There is not much more to say. The bartender has your soup ready, sets a free draw next to it because he knows these people and you have played along. When you ask, he is happy to unlock the gas pumps so you can be on your way.

Another kind of confrontation is less problematic. When I turned back to see who was tugging at my sleeve in the middle of the University of Washington's Red Square, I didn't see anyone. Then she tugged again, bowing beneath my elbow: a tiny Japanese schoolgirl, or so I assumed, given her uniform. She held up her camera and pointed at it and then at me—*OK?* the question posed by her eyebrows. Thinking that she wanted me to take her picture, I nodded and framed her in my mind's eye before the red brick buildings and the Seattle skyline—black buckled walking shoes, white kneesocks, pleated skirt, white blouse and blue jacket, bobbed black hair, and that smile.

But when I reached for her camera, she shook her head and pointed at me again. My defenses went up. She wanted a picture of me. I was the site. I was the souvenir. But she was cute, and charmed by her blushing, her self-effacing manners and courage, I was easily disarmed. This girl had singled me out, or so I thought, and I nodded again. On display, I would hold a studied pose, framed by the red brick of the University of Washington. What could it hurt: an odd couple for a moment, each contrasting the other in size and nationality? But I understood only partially. Then she turned and said something I didn't understand, and from behind a corner, fourteen Japanese schoolgirls swarmed at me.

America is a big place full of totems. My recruiter backed up, fiddling with the lens, and then swept her hand left and right and talked fast. My flock lined up shoulder to shoulder on both sides of me and faced her like blackbirds on a cedar branch. I stood, dumbfounded, in the middle.

East and west I saw the tops of heads one by one in descending heights, seven to a side, and I thought, *why not?* If there was the slightest mix-up about who we were, it could be answered with a shrug. Odd, comic, our differences felt worthy of celebration. I held my arms straight out, palms forward, over three heads each way and smiled. It took awhile to compose fifteen pictures, each new photographer looking through her viewfinder and laughing as the absurd lineup came into focus. Maybe one of them is chuckling right now as she sips tea and leafs through her old photo album to find herself in line, with the tall man at the center, everyone in the picture so young as she looks up thirty-odd years later and out her window at the green springtime gardens of Kyoto.

° ° °

I REALIZE THAT I HAVE LEFT THE OUTCOME OF OUR GAME AGAINST Oregon State literally up in the air. We are still behind by one point with seconds to go.

The noise was incredible in Slats Gill Coliseum, eleven thousand voices compressing the court, time dropping second by second. In my replay, Loy Peterson is still reaching up behind him as the ball spins slowly out of the lights. Launching myself toward him, body parallel to the oak floor, I knew that the ball and Loy Peterson and I would arrive at the same place in the universe at approximately the same time. Given a turn and a little more effort, I could have reached the ball first. I know that now. But before my coaches on the bench and my mother and father, six rows up, rise to defend me, let me confess: I chose to whack Loy Peterson.

Maybe it was my "atavistic" impulses, or my "outlaw" or "nonlaw" self, as Oates puts it; or perhaps, like Richard Ford, I was "all unwholesome violence inside," because the collision—head, forearm, shoulder—felt wonderful. I did nothing to avoid it, and of course had thought nothing about the consequences of such a wreck.

The results were pathetic. Grunting in pain, the air whooshing from our lungs, both of us smashed to the floor, and then a puff of air in my left ear, almost sweet, as if someone had whispered something to me. I tried to stand, Loy Peterson on top of me, flailing. As near as I can figure, that puff of air must have been Peterson's fist flying by my ear. I felt lucky he had missed, and I held on, grabbed him under the arms in a clinch, a bear hug that had no affection about it, and stood up, lifting him off the ground. I remember the officials waving, spit flying from their whistles, the coaches' ties flapping, the benches emptying, but I wasn't letting go of Peterson, because the first thing I saw over his shoulder was Oregon State's Harry Gunner, a six foot five, 230-pound football tight end—hatchet-man sub-and-fixer for the basketball team during the winter—scrabbling straight for me with his fist cocked. All I could think was to hold Loy Peterson in my arms, moving him left then right, a little dance of self-preservation. Peterson made a fine shield. And then it was over.

With ten seconds left in the game, both of us were ejected. Our team lost by two points, so someone from Oregon State must have sunk one of the two free throws awarded for my flagrant foul. Security guards had escorted me to the locker room. The benches settled down. Neither of my coaches mentioned it after the game. Later at the hotel, my father shook his head, as if he had seen this before. My mother asked, what was I thinking?

The truth is I wasn't thinking. If I said that I gave my body up for the Cougars, my welfare for the game, or said that I fought against "inequity" and for "justice," these would be afterthoughts at best, excuses at worst. At full speed and three feet off the ground, the ball just out of reach, I gave up the discipline of basketball to indulge the primitive. That's it. Misdemeanor assault. I felt speechless and pitiful until the next night, when we played the University of Oregon at Eugene, and then I felt like a villain.

"Who you gonna hit tonight, McKean?" someone yelled from the crowd as we warmed up in McArthur Court on the Oregon campus. "Hey, forty-two. Hey, bully."

When I was introduced, the boos rolled long and thunderous. I didn't care. For some reason, I felt proud, maybe even a little sinister. *So this is what those wrestlers feel, the real villains.* I remember the crowd on their feet and roaring during the game as Oregon made a run at us, but I turned, fading, and sank a long jump shot to pull us ahead. The crowd noise fell off as if someone had hit a switch. I sat them back down and relished the denial of it.

Relished it all the way home to Pullman. Given the attention, I probably thought I was a bona fide tough guy, that is until the first practice Monday after my infamous weekend in Oregon. There on my locker for all to see hung a pair of boxing gloves. Pinned to them was a note in pencil on lined paper, the hand as crabbed as a broken nose: "McKean—You need help. Come see me.—Deeter."

ONE-ON-ONE

ABOUT THE SIZE OF A TOILET-PAPER ROLL, THE WHITE CARD-board tube—a thick, green fuse taped along its length—felt a little heavier than a baseball. Printed on the side in army font was "Hand Grenade Simulator," above the warning "Do Not Ignite Within 15 Feet of Anything Flammable." On a warm summer night in 1969, at one in the morning on the sleepy, half-deserted campus in Pullman, Washington, I pulled the fuse cap and threw what my friend Jane called a "big firecracker" off the roof of the Sigma Nu house into an alley. I watched over the edge like Kilroy, with Jane at my side and our friend Duncan, who had been assigned to look after his empty fraternity house all summer, himself the only ROTC English-summer-school graduate, student-deferred cadet at Washington State University with a beard and shoulder-length red hair covering his ears.

If I had thought about it beforehand, a fifteen-foot radius means a thirty-foot flash, but the tube and its sizzle had already plopped onto the gravel. Then exploded. Filled every sense, ears boxed and ringing, breath blown out, a slap in the face, my eyes pit-ted with orange and red, two bright circles I saw everywhere I looked. The echo of bludgeoned air rolled down the campus hill into Pullman. No toy did that to your heart.

We hid for an hour or so, watching a police cruiser circle the block, washing its searchlight across the empty fraternities and sororities. Frightened and exhilarated, I tried to see, through the red circles fading in my retinas, if we had blown out the windows in the sorority house next door. Then at 2:30, having learned nothing, we tried the flare. I removed the cap with its firing pin from the top of the tube, placed it on the bottom where the primer shell was, held the tube pointed up and out, slapped the cap with my hand, and fired the flare, which rocketed high over the Victorian house of the university president. There in green light lay his tidy backyard: swings, a goldfish pond, and manicured evergreens. Beyond his iron fence, a small park and run-down neighborhood of old houses. Hung beneath its parachute, the burning phosphorus fell for a long time, eerie and surreal, casting more shadow than light, giving fear enough time to show itself, I imagined, before the dark filled in.

Where Jane got these things I didn't know, but she had given them to me—not to symbolize our relationship, as I probably thought once, but because they scared her. They meant Vietnam to her. She had seen what such things lead to. Kind, affectionate, and dutiful to her friends, Jane had gathered me in as her new friend that summer, me the ex–basketball star at loose ends, lost between my playing past and what I might do for a living in the future. We had known each other at a distance as undergraduates at Washington State University, but then we lost contact when I went abroad to play, briefly, for a washing-machine factory in Bologna, Italy, and then for the Gillette All-Stars, a touring team made up of American players suspended in the great hardwood purgatory between college basketball and the NBA. It was temporary work, I realize now, but having focused so intently on basketball all those years, I couldn't see clearly where I had been, and certainly not where I was going. That is, until I was momentarily blinded that summer in Pullman, and Jane helped me to see.

On the roof she said, "John Nebel told me the white tube was like a big firecracker. He's back from Vietnam. In the hospital, you know, at Madigan in Tacoma."

"I didn't know," I said, too surprised and ashamed just then to explain I hadn't even known he was in Vietnam. He had been a teammate for two years, the first year in 1964 on our undefeated freshman basketball team at WSU, and the next year when we both played for the varsity.

"I think he'd like to see you," she said.

John starred at Mercer Island High School near Seattle when I was playing for Wilson High School in Tacoma. As classmates the next year at WSU, we both flunked the Royal Canadian Air Force physical fitness exam to become the only two scholarship-holding basketball players assigned to remedial freshman PE. Read out loud and mispronounced, our names were among the twelve singled out of sixty in line in baggy shorts and acceptable PE T-shirts to report to the conditioning room because we had been found "unfit." Maybe three pull-ups didn't pass, but John and I protested injustice or a coaching conspiracy for weeks, while twelve odd body shapes sailed nowhere in rowing machines or lifted dumbbells or ran the daily laps around the perimeter of the gym, in the middle of which forty-eight examples of military fitness whacked at badminton birdies. There is nothing like mutual humiliation to promote teamwork, and John and I were good teammates for those two years. But by his junior year he had quit the team, and we drifted apart, he to his studies and the Army ROTC, and I almost single-mindedly to basketball.

When Jane asked me the next day if I would like to see John in the hospital, I said yes, though I was immediately anxious, even frightened. She mentioned how he had been close to a howitzer-shell booby trap, how devastating the shrapnel. My ears still hurt from the explosion the night before, but I couldn't imagine what he had come back from and how badly he had been injured. Why was I afraid? I had no idea what to expect or what he might expect of me. I had made little effort to keep in touch with John, and given even less credence to the war. What would my wandering through Europe mean to him, or the two years he had missed playing at WSU? Would he want to hear about my playing against Lew Alcindor, the loss and frustration, how our old coach explained the matchup by saying McKean's "the one who played against Alcindor. That's why I said Alcindor must have been 7'6", because McKean would stand by him and Alcindor's arm would be on McKean's shoulder." Did the lop-sided contest have anything to do with John's experiences? Was it guilt I was feeling?

As Jane and I traveled across Washington State, three hundred miles from Pullman to Tacoma's Madigan Hospital, I took with me the image of John Nebel sprinting full court in a game we played against Montana in Missoula: A defensive rebound falls my way, I turn, and there's John just past the ten-second line on his way down court. I throw a football pass, leading him, and he catches it over his shoulder, dribbles once, and lays it in.

My concept of the Vietnam War was and still is ambiguous, burlesque, and carnival-like in the extreme. Neither *dulce* nor *decorum,* the language and images I have collected for the war clash—a Buddhist monk's self-immolation on a Saigon street on the same stage in my mind as the graduate art student in Pullman who, hating the war, painted himself in indelible ink, Adam's apple to shaved toes, as Captain America. His art friends helped, great graphic illustrators that they were, and detailed him down to the shoelaces and stitches. He covered his true identity with a three-piece suit, got a buzz haircut and a briefcase, and reported to his Army physical. Word has it he disappeared behind the door marked "psychological exam." Or a friend from high school who showed me the huge scar next to his right shoulder blade and, laughing as if such bravado were commonplace, said someone shot him as he ran as fast as he could out of the jungle. Or the stories circulated about a high school classmate who had volunteered for the infantry, shipped out, and soon after he arrived in Vietnam, jumped over a log and onto a land mine. For us he was simply no longer there, his name fading as if we knew his story better than we had known him—how despite warnings not to, his father had opened the sealed casket to see what was left of his son.

° ° °

FOR ME, ARMY BUSINESS ON CAMPUS WAS A LONG WAY OFF. I would watch from the top row of seats in the empty football stadium—running the steps was a mandatory preseason basketball conditioner—as the miniature ROTC cadets marched in the fields next to Bohler Gym, all that order barking and square corners, the creases and spit-polished shoes bobbing and turning in unison. At home in the summer of 1965, I found the Army fifteen miles south of Tacoma at Fort Lewis, an immense training center and jumping-off spot for Vietnam. I would roll up to the gate, talk my way past the guards, basketball and gear on the front seat. Then I would stand around in the base gym until the soldiers invited me to play in their pickup games. It seemed like a fair trade-off. I was a good freshman college player who could shoot, and they were strong and enthusiastic. It was the physical game I was after, and the soldiers played hard, ragged basketball. They were serious and granted authority to skill—a good move, a fadeaway jumper that found only net. "Good shot," they would say. "What else can you do?" Despite the charley horses and bloody knees, the squint of a bruised eye, this was what I wanted to hear, that I had stood up and endured, that I could play the game.

But Fort Lewis was too neatly oppressive, all that olive drab, those painted rocks, the shiny recruits in clean uniforms marching down the roads, the other less polished soldiers I remembered seeing, alone or in pairs, sunburned and taciturn, watching from the edges as if they had something incredible pressing on their minds. There was static in the air, and boredom at the same time, if that is possible. Somebody knew something and wasn't talking. I remember after one pickup game, when I felt strong and cocky from scoring over twenty points, a black sergeant asked me how old I was, fifteen? Something was being tested. I wasn't sure what the stakes were, but I knew the game was serious. Even when I returned to school, there was the Vietnam War in all its contradictions: the protests on campus, the magazines with their galleries of dead, friends leaving for Canada or Brazil, others leaving for Vietnam. Some came back unable to sleep, loving guns and solitude.

In the fall of 1966, the Army drew very close to me—too close. WSU had been in session only a few weeks, and the basketball team had begun its conditioning programs and first practices when I got my draft papers in the mail. The salutation really said "Greetings," and the body of the letter ordered me to report to Spokane in early December for a physical. This can't be right, I thought, for all the self-serving reasons, and I went to the Selective Service office on campus and discovered that the "satisfactory student progress" computer card I had filled out during fall registration had been rejected, its information never sent to the draft board in Tacoma to verify that I was, indeed, a student. I had written the wrong figures in the little box marked "draft number." What a petty detail, I thought, and even though the campus office sent off a correctly filled-in form, I still visited the draft board in Tacoma a week later to make sure. An elderly lady behind the counter two steep flights up at 915½ Pacific Avenue in Tacoma asked if she could help. I laid the summons paper on the counter and explained—not so well, I might add—that I was supposed to be in Ohio to play basketball against Ohio State in December, and in January we were playing UCLA and Lew Alcindor, whom she must have heard of, and alas, I didn't have time to take this physical. She broke her poignant silence by thumping shut a large leather-spined book into which she had, undoubtedly, recorded my name. I have seen her likeness recently in Grant Wood's painting *Daughters of the Revolution.* White hair severely pulled back, a sweater buttoned up but having no effect on the chill in her expression, and wire glasses through which she sees through me, perfectly.

"There are boys in Vietnam who haven't got time to be there either," she said—words I can still hear—and then she asked to see my draft card and my Notice of Classification card. Rummaging through my wallet, I could find neither. She led me, still rummaging, to a table behind her counter and set before me a sheet of paper that listed the years in jail I faced and the dollar amount in fines imposed for not carrying these two cards on my person.

Aware of the gravity by now, I found the cards, though no more words to explain myself. I shrugged my shoulders, an old response to the humiliations of grade school—this chair as stiff-backed as those outside the principal's office, where more than once I came to attention, owned up, and paid my dues. When another woman, middle-aged, approached with a file and asked me if I was McKean, I almost raised my hand. "Yes," I said, and stood. She explained that they had finally received my student-progress information, then hesitated and asked, "By the way, Clayton, how tall are you?"

"Six foot ten," I hedged.

"Well," she said with a shrug, "you're not regulation. You can thumb your nose at us if you like. And if we bother you again, have your physician send us a note as to your height."

My trial took ten minutes. Weightless all the way down the stairs, blessed by the extraordinary, I was untouchable. No one else had ever called me by my middle name, and her doing so seemed the gavel stroke on my liberation from the conventional, from draft papers and roll calls and basic training, from the category of the common soldier. My only uniform would serve basketball. She had freed me, I thought at the time, from the specter of Vietnam. Odd man out, abnormal, and beyond reach were defined by the Army as simply "nonregulation" and therefore without existence. How ironic and dark and comic and nebulous that seemed to me in 1966.

° ° °

I WANTED TO EXPLAIN TO JOHN NEBEL THAT THE ONLY THING clear to me at that time was that we would play UCLA in Pullman on January 7. The defining moment was less than three months away, and the thought of it was like a set of blinders. He would understand that we had a good-enough team, although eccentric and a bit of a throwback. Every player came from somewhere in the state of Washington. We had two miniature guards, Lenny Allen at five foot nine and Ray Stein at five foot eleven, known in Pullman as the "Dynamic Duo," who had their own fan club and buttons. Our forwards were built like tight ends, Randy Stoll at six foot seven and 235, Ted Wierman at six foot eight and 240, and Bud Norris—who really did play tight end—at six foot four and 235, and whose credentials included knocking Cazzie Russell unconscious in our game against Michigan in the Far West Classic Basketball Tournament in Portland, Oregon. Despite Bud's downfield defense, Russell's layup was good, and he managed to score thirty more points after he regained his senses.

I was the center at six foot nine, and "scrawny," to quote coach Marv Harshman. In some ways, we were the perfect example of a "balanced" basketball team. Fast and slow at the same time, we ran patterns that would release our two little guards down the court, the ball never touching the ground. Some teams we simply overwhelmed by our good block-and-tackle technique, others by the speed of our guards. As disciplined as an army squad, we ran well-drilled patterns and waited for our opportunities. In appearance we were the perfect WSU team—a group of stable, conservative young men who could have been plowing the good deep soil of eastern Washington instead of playing ball.

But UCLA presented a problem, to understate the issue. They were New York players via L.A. Neither our coaches nor our players could conceive of the dimensions of UCLA's game, or duplicate them with a practice team. Extraordinary measures were needed. The coaches taped a three-foot board to forward Dick Jacob's arm, and he swatted away our layups and jump shots until we were all gun-shy. I remember tennis rackets, too. At Alcindor's post position, Dick Watters stood on a fourteen-inch stool and held the ball out of everyone's reach. All this made for good copy, the *Tacoma News Tribune* running pictures and an article under the caption "WSU Becomes Stool Pigeon For Big Lew." In the photo, I look like the smallest kid in a neighborhood pickup game, standing on tiptoes and peeking up at the boosted Watters, who is calling for the ball once more. It is the same look I have in the photos of the real game. The article quotes Harshman as saying, "Many of the kids on our team haven't seen Alcindor and can't imagine how much area he covers, how agile he is, and how much damage he can do." Then he explains that the difficulty in playing against Alcindor is the "psychological effect he creates, particularly in the shooting department."

We couldn't leap as high, nor run as fast for as long, and the psychological effect encompassed far more than shooting. Conventional advice to a team is to play their own game, that players are skilled in what they practice over and over, but Lew Alcindor—the whole UCLA team, for that matter—forced us to play a new game, to operate in dimensions we weren't familiar with and many times couldn't reach. We couldn't practice what we couldn't imagine, and the slapstick of tennis rackets and stools helped only a little.

Despite what Harshman said, many of us had seen Lew Alcindor play in Los Angeles the year before, when the UCLA freshman team played in a preliminary game. We knew who we were facing, but not quite what to expect, and that became a preoccupation. I allowed him far too much space in my own head, thinking of him for weeks during study evenings in WSU's Holland Library. I remember my hands sweating, but nothing that I may have read. I thought of him during my pregame dressing superstitions: left ankle taped first, then right; left shoe tied first, then right—and during the two-flight climb up the darkened stairway, past the chlorine smell of the pool, past the crowd and the cigarette smoke in the lobby, and then our pushing through the open double doors into the glare and noise, the crowd on its feet and the band starting up.

Though it cannot compare with John's long journey into the jungle, my anticipation of the game still comes back with power—the preparation and brooding in the quiet basement of Bohler Gym, the diagrams on the blackboard, the potential fakes and moves, the choreography, the imagined shots going up and in. Then the game in the mind melts into the game at hand, as thought and action coincide beneath the bright lights.

That evening, I carried Lew Alcindor up the stairs with me. During the warm-up drills, I tried to keep my mind on my own business—the game was twenty minutes away, and the people in the crowd, some of whom had waited for days for seats in Bohler Gym, oohed and aahed in disbelief, slapped their collective foreheads, and whistled between their teeth—but curiosity got the best of me. I still see over my shoulder the powder blue of the UCLA team at their end of the court and Lew Alcindor in line for layups. At his turn, he dribbles twice and rises up in the most elementary move in basketball—leaping off the left foot, right knee up, right hand reaching—and pins the basketball against the backboard six inches above the shooting square, over twelve feet up. And lets go. Then and now, a ballet master would compliment his "elevation" and a poet admire the wonderful sense of understatement, the ball dropping through the net as Alcindor jogs to the end of the rebounding line.

I shouldn't have been watching. There was no time for analogies; describing the game and playing it require two different states of mind. Appointed to guard Lew Alcindor—or sacrificed, depending on your point of view—I needed to warm up. Play, don't watch; watching is too slow, always half a step behind. But the awe and fear and simple admiration turned my head.

We had a strategy, though, and it almost worked. We thought we could force UCLA out of its game plan with our defense, and with the help of the noisy crowd stuffed into our cracker-box gym, five thousand fans in four thousand seats. My assignment was simple: I had to occupy Alcindor's favored spot before he could get there. Pregame films showed us that he liked to set up along the right side of the key about halfway toward the foul line; after we lost possession or scored, I ran hard to get back first. When he came down and turned and tried to back his way into position, I would push and block to keep him out. Or I would push and release and step in front, always trying to upset his timing and change his game. Sometimes it worked; he wasn't as strong as I thought he would be. Other times I would try to time the pass, playing the passing lane, defending against the forward, who might raise the ball over his head, look at Alcindor, and then pass. Those were easy to pick off.

A few of my offensive moves worked too. When posting up during the first half, I could see in my peripheral vision that Alcindor had his arms down or out to the side, even when I had the ball in deep. My turnaround fadeaway jump shot wasn't working at all, so one time I tried a turnaround shot, jumping up and in quickly. I concentrated on the setup more than I aimed at the basket—elbows in, one hand beneath, the other behind and up on the ball—so that I had the shot positioned right above the top of his forehead. He couldn't get his hands up in time, and I had only to follow through to make my short eight-footer go in. Simple. I surprised him another time when I received the ball near our foul line as our team moved to set up. As the center on our team, I wasn't supposed to be that high in the key, but I turned to face the basket anyway, and there was Alcindor moving quickly from beneath the basket. I could see by the look on his face that he was eager to make a point, to serve me lunch by stuffing the ball back where it came from. All I had to do was fake the shot from there—a little basketball sleight of hand, a one-syllable lie, my head, the ball, and my shoulders all in on it—and up he went. In my imagination I can see his shoes going by, but all I remember is an easy layup after one dribble.

What I don't remember is any of these moves working more than once. Not because they were ineffective or accidental, but because Lew Alcindor was a smart, aware, analytical player, who read his opponents well and adjusted quickly. Although deceptive, a little quicker than he was, and faster to the floor, I was not that complicated a text.

By some quirk and a little luck, however, we were ahead early in the second half, mostly because Alcindor was in foul trouble. When the ball was thrown to him in the post, he had a tendency to hook me with his left arm and roll into his shot. I couldn't hope to reach the ball, so I held my position. As the game progressed, I moved more resolutely into his path so the hooking might seem even more pronounced. Add a little stagger, I thought, a little reel, and perhaps the official would see a smaller man being bullied by the bigger, more famous guy from L.A. It was a good theory that worked a couple of times.

When Alcindor committed his fourth foul with twelve minutes left in the second half, he was taken out, and the next four-and-a-half minutes were ecstatic, as if all was right with the world. The game now at my level, I shot the ball over their second-string center, rebounded, and tipped one in. No more drought. No more famine. We regained control of ourselves as well as the game, and pulled ahead by one point with nine-and-a-half minutes left. Joy, oh, joy; pass me the ball.

All too soon, Alcindor was back. They slowed the game down to prevent his fouling out and worked through our defense for close shot after close shot. On offense, we became hesitant once again, stricken by second thoughts. For me, one play shows how tenuous my threat was to Alcindor. Given the ball near the foul lane, I turned to find that he had dropped off, leaving me room to shoot. I put a lot of arch on the ball, but he jumped, reached, and just nicked the ball with his fingertips before it reached its peak and fell neatly with a swish through the basket. I had the two points, but felt as though he had made the basket. After that, the rest of my shots seemed like improvisations, each a variation I had never practiced. This is exactly the goal of good defense—don't go for the grand gesture or the dramatic rejection, but simply force the other team into unfamiliar territory, where they have no skill, comfort, or confidence. We played well and lost by nine points, the closest we ever came to beating Lew Alcindor's UCLA.

After that first game, we couldn't help feeling frustrated and optimistic at the same time. "What was he like?" my roommates asked. They had waited all night for good seats and found them two rows behind the end line. "Did you hear us yelling at you?" No, I couldn't see them for the bright lights, and couldn't hear them in the incomprehensible roar and din beyond the out-of-bounds lines. Inside those lines, the absorption in the moment was absolute, and only afterward in scenes and tableaux did the event begin to show itself. Perhaps it wasn't until February 17, 1967, when *Life Magazine* featured in its sports section the article "Big Lew Measures His Lonely World," that I understood the dimensions of his game. On page 106 beneath the full-page photograph, the caption reads: "In an out-of-town game against Washington State, Lew springs past State's 6-foot-9-inch center Jim McKean and deftly curls in a basket." My father cut the photo out and kept it in a scrapbook. For years I remembered myself in this photo as being *contained* by Alcindor, a word normally used to describe what a good defender does to an offensive player. I remembered jumping as high as I could, my feet higher off the floor than Alcindor's, my reach far less, my hand slapping at his elbow.

I have three copies of that issue now, bought at shopping malls when they host antique dealers in the walkways. The last dealer sold me a copy for ten bucks and raised his eyebrows when I showed him page 106 and said that was me. My memory gives me more credit than I'm due, however, for the picture shows me simply out-jumped, my feet far below Alcindor's. Looking straight up, I have my mouth open, as does much of the crowd, given that the ball in his hand is ten inches above the basket. The antique dealer said that anytime I wanted a mint copy to let him know, and I will, for it contains articles and pictures that illustrate not only the dimensions of Lew Alcindor's game but the dimensions of time as well.

In that same issue, there are poems by, and an article about, the Russian poet Yevgeny Yevtushenko and his visit to America. There is a dismissive article about the "Other Culture," the one that celebrates "happenings" and performance art, and claims poets as its kings and William Burroughs's *Naked Lunch* as its bible, which all seem a little corny now. There is an article about a doctor volunteering to help the villagers in Vietnam, a kind of Tom Dooley, "The 'Bac Si' from Iowa." One of the subtitles in the article reads: "A volunteer M.D. wars on pain in Vietnam."

Elsewhere in this issue, *Life Magazine* fans the smoldering public argument over the war. In the "Presidency" section, Hugh Sidey quotes Lyndon Johnson as saying, "I chase every peace feeler just like my little beagle chases a squirrel." In the book review section, Webster Schott claims that Robert Lowell's *Near the Ocean* consolidates his literary position, that his poems have "documented the U.S. intellectual's painful travel through recent time." Schott quotes Lowell:

> *Pity the planet, all joy gone*
> *from this sweet volcanic cone;*
> *peace to our children when they fall*
> *in small war on the heels of small*
> *war—until the end of time*
> *to police the earth, a ghost*
> *orbiting forever lost*
> *in the monotonous sublime.*

What a contrast those lines give to the comforting images of healing and the refrain of "peace" in this issue of *Life.* Lowell suggests that the price of war is simply and horribly the loss of our children until the earth itself is a ghost. The whole era seems clearly revealed in these pages: how the counterculture and the poets understood enough to protest the war; how the public was fed images of healing and the language of peace; and how, finally, Johnson's predatory simile suggests a more chilling truth, a government strategy to chase down peace and kill it.

When I reread the excerpt from Lowell's poem, I think of my friend John Nebel walking down a path in Vietnam, on a mission the government called a "police action." And because I wasn't there, my frames of reference are from basketball, from what I have read, and from a walk I once took in Costa Rica. Following a path, narrow and dark, overgrown and lush, into a cloud forest, I imagine John walking before me with his pack and an M-16, almost a full court's length ahead, and when he turns to hear something I say, the sudden light beneath his feet burns the leaves and shines through him, the delayed thump like a fist knocking him to the ground. That year, 1969, we were both twenty-three, but I was still trying to understand my life in terms of a game.

I remember another frigid Wednesday evening in February of 1967, when I sat in Holland Library and couldn't focus on anything but the coming weekend. On Thursday we would drive, on ice-covered roads in subzero weather, the seventy-eight miles north to Spokane, get on a plane, and fly to Los Angeles. Still wearing our overcoats and boots—stunned by the sun, palm trees, and warm Pacific salt air—we would be driven to the Miramar Hotel in Santa Monica. The stunning had only begun: we were to play USC on Friday night and UCLA on Saturday night.

We beat USC, 86 to 76, but lost to UCLA, 100 to 78—not a surprising margin. Sitting on the bench late in the game with a towel draped over my head, I could easily see the source of our catastrophe: Lew Alcindor's domination. Before Pauley Pavilion's suntanned crowd, mugged even by UCLA's band, which sat at floor level and bleated raspberries at me every time I ran past, I had become a statistical anomaly. In the March 1968 issue of *Sport* magazine, Coach Harshman is quoted as saying: "My center, Jim McKean, told me after the game, 'Coach, I may go into the record books as the guy who let Alcindor get 61, but you'll be known as the coach who was dumb enough to play him man-to-man.'" I don't remember feeling especially witty then, so maybe John McCallum got it right in his historical survey, *College Basketball U.S.A. Since 1892,* published in 1978, where Harshman's statement is given like this: "I said, 'So tonight we're going to play one-on-one against Alcindor.' Jim McKean, a scrawny 6'8" kid from Tacoma, was my center. I said, 'Jim, you're probably going to go down in history as the guy who held Alcindor to maybe 50 points, and I'll go down as the coach who was dumb enough to match you one-on-one with him.'" I had grown shorter and thinner in the intervening ten years, and would soon fade completely. Between the opening jump and the final buzzer, Lew Alcindor made his point *and* his points, scoring twenty-two in the last four minutes in great sweeping moves to the basket. Sixty-one points. It was magnificent and humiliating. My pride badly wounded, I had fouled out early in the second half.

What began to change that evening, as I sat at the far end of the bench, was my view of the game. As firsthand witness to a redefinition of basketball by a great player, I became "regulation" once again, given perspective and my own ordinary mortality back. It sounds like a story by Jack London: sitting on a bench and crying after his final loss, the old boxer thought he had the younger man down for good in the first round, but the kid got up on the count of eight . . .

The next year, as we traveled to play teams in Berkeley, Los Angeles, and Seattle, I was able to see a larger, more disturbing picture of the time I was playing in. After spending one afternoon before the California game walking up Telegraph Avenue, the new culture everywhere in dress and music, I stood in Sproul Plaza on the Berkeley campus, dressed in my gray slacks and crimson Cougar blazer, as a crowd formed on the steps and a neatly dressed black man spoke, in increasing volume, about burning whitey out of his stores, how blacks should rise up for freedom and power. His name was Stokely Carmichael, and he frightened me—not because of the suggested violence, but because I understood for a moment how the conventional fell short. Frightened for my own loss of ignorance, I knew there were many changes in store. To recall Lowell, there were "small wars" going on even here, with many lives at stake. Even Lew Alcindor was a symbol to be discarded to the past, and Kareem Abdul-Jabbar the more appropriate and significant name to take into the future.

When I tried to explain this change later to the poet William Stafford, how the world seemed more complex and issues more urgent than my basketball games, he alluded to Corinthians, saying that perhaps I had put away "childish things." Visiting John Nebel helped me to sort out and, in some ways, define those basketball years. On the way to Madigan Hospital outside of Tacoma, Jane explained what she knew, how John had been second in line on patrol, how the point man had tripped the howitzer-shell booby trap and died, how John had been devastated by shrapnel, his right leg gone below the knee, his torso full of holes, his jaw broken, his right ear blown out, his larynx cut.

"He can't hear well and can only whisper, so speak up when you see him. Don't whisper," she said as we found our way to Madigan Hospital and parked. She had been there before and knew of a side door that opened into a long corridor. We walked for a long time, in dim light and disinfectant smell. In remarkable quiet, we pushed through double doors into a darkened ward, and there behind a screen and beneath a bright light lay John Nebel.

° ° °

WHAT COMPLETED MY CHANGE IN VISION WEREN'T THE QUARTER-size scars he showed me, or the splints for the fingers in his left hand, or the half cast on his left foot and the new bandage just below his right knee, though I was stunned and sorry.

"Six five, and only 160 pounds made it back," he said. His leg hurt, I could see, but he explained how he was carried into the helicopter, how soldiers were on top of him, how he was yelling, "My legs, my legs." How he spent hazy time in the hospital in Japan. And pointing to the pictures on the stand beside his bed, his parents' home on Mercer Island, his boat, he explained how he would water-ski again with his girlfriend, how these were the places he had left and was on his way back to. Struck and near tears, I was convinced because he was convinced. "I didn't lose anything I need," he said, asking the nurse, who stopped by, for a jug to pee in. "Things still work where they count."

And it wasn't the shot of morphine the nurse gave him, his leg having been operated on the day before, the gauze seeping, and the pain obvious in his face. Nor was it any conclusion I drew on the way home, Jane silent in the passenger seat, looking at the rain-glazed lights along South Tacoma Avenue. No comparisons worked. I had played a game, the point of which was to contain or be contained. If I had ever thought the language of sports, the metaphors themselves, might serve as a way to understand my friend John's experience, I was wrong. The shrapnel went through him, as if he wasn't there. Perhaps that is the awful point. Basketball gives definition to all its players, even those who lose; but war takes definition away—it undefines, erases, reduces even the best of its players to shattered ruin or a scattering of ashes. Even to do poorly in basketball is to be held, and whole.

And finally, it wasn't our saying goodbye and not talking until years later, though I regret we haven't kept in touch. No. What really completed my change in vision is the shame I recall of not remembering what Jane had asked me to do, before she and I stepped into the bright light beside John's bed and I fumbled for his good hand, when he asked in a strained, raspy voice, "How are you?"

"Speak up," she had said.

But I whispered. "Fine. Thanks. I'm fine."

CANDY

Someone in Prairie Lights Bookstore in Iowa City was wearing English Leather aftershave. It was December 1998, and standing by the poetry section, I immediately thought of my mother changing the sheets of my bed at three in the morning as I slumped in a chair in the corner of the bedroom I grew up in. That was thirty years ago. All she said was "OK," and "back to bed." In another three hours the fever would break again.

Maybe her doctor, another in my mother's stable of osteopaths, had wafted English Leather over me as he explained the vagaries of mononucleosis and adjusted my neck. I remember trying to walk fast enough past the anonymous knees in his waiting room and out the clinic doors so the world would stop disappearing—a little here, a little up there in the corner, then the lower half evaporating, black field bleeding into black field. A flutter of coats and quick steps behind me, my mother caught up as I bent over in the parking lot like a kid playing turtle and rested on my hands. "Go get the car, please," I said. "Just go get the car."

Back came the world in pieces, just as it does in memory. Reassembled in bed, I couldn't move. It took weeks to read Hunter

Thompson's *Hell's Angels,* each page weighing a pound. The phone rang and rang. It had to be Milan, but I was going nowhere.

In Prairie Lights I forgot what I had come for and looked instead for a copy of Thompson's *Hell's Angels.* The memory of 1968 was all over the store. Vonnegut and Kenneth Patchen. *The Journal of Albion Moonlight* rushed back. Steppenwolf, incense, mono, *The Electric Kool-Aid Acid Test,* the Quicksilver Messenger Company. Italy calling. Where is he?

In the spring of 1968, I had agreed to play for an Italian basketball team, Candy, in Bologna. They offered to find me an apartment, lend me a car, and pay a salary. But now, in late August, they kept calling to find out why I hadn't arrived. My mother leaned through my bedroom door to say, "They want to know when you can come." Five weeks later, in a warehouse in Milan, I posed in a Candy jersey, standing between two washing machines, a basketball in each hand, arms out over the top loaders as if the basketballs needed a wash cycle or two. I still have that promo picture where I stand straight up, emaciated and wide-eyed, above the lids of the open machines.

A month after I arrived, and to my great disappointment, Candy pawned me off to the Gillette All-Stars, a team of vagabond ex-college players coached by the American Jim McGregor, who knew more about self-promotion and backroom deals than coaching basketball. How did I end up handing out razor blades and shaving cream and "Look Sharp, Be Sharp" pennants to full-time auto mechanics or teachers or accountants who played basketball three nights a week for teams somewhere in Tuscany or León or Ljubljana? I have wondered for years.

On occasion, I have groused about this mysterious turnabout to Jim Harris, the owner of Prairie Lights, perched behind his computer at the back of the store. An enthusiastic and knowledgeable sports fan, Jim has been curious for a long time about my short-lived playing career in Europe. I have never had much to tell him, not being sure of the whole story myself. I can remember a piece here and there: how Candy held practice in the Palazzo dello Sport, how I wandered by myself warm evenings through the streets of Bologna, how the Gillette team played once on the second floor of a very old building on a canal in Venice, the fans seated with their backs to the frescoes. So finally, on that day in December, Jim sent me to the "Travel" section: Italy. Knopf Guides to Bologna and Venice. As I thumbed through them, Jim showed me a book by Antonio Salvadori entitled *A Guide to the Principal Buildings of Venice.* On page 105, under entry number 59, I found a picture and description of "Scuola Nuova Misericordia," a two-story building designed by Jacopo Sansovino and built between 1523 and 1583.

"At present, the ground floor is used as a warehouse, and the upper floor as a gymnasium," the description says. Yes. That was the entrance, and those were the stairs leading up from the canal where our water taxi unloaded ten American basketball players. The Gillette All-Stars had played there, and I knew, standing in Prairie Lights, that Italy held answers for me, that I had to go back and see.

° ° °

THIS IS MILANO CALLING. IS HE COMING YET? YES, MY MOTHER COULD finally say. Seattle to Newark, Newark to Milan, I slept most of the way and then waited, bags in hand, in the Milan airport for someone to pick me up. Two men with thin moustaches stepped up in their trench coats. Could you possibly be Signore McKean, the rebounder, the force in the middle? their tipped-back Homburgs and puzzled looks seemed to ask.

My escorts found me a hotel room so I could rest for a few hours. Now, to my physical reduction—I had lost fifteen pounds—I added culture shock and linguistic losses. That morning in a Milan hotel, I felt like Columbus washed up on the far side of Jamaica, bewildered, his hull worm shot. I soon discovered that Candy was a washing machine factory, and a bidet was neither a foot wash nor a urinal. Though it worked for both. *Pronto,* I was supposed to say into the telephone, and *dove* meant where the hell was I? That evening, their Mercedes hummed at 160 kilometers an hour down a freeway toward Bologna. How the driver saw the trucks in front of us still amazes me. Two flicks of the high beams, and we zipped by the canvas-flapped and multiwheeled behemoths crawling in the outside lane.

° ° °

IN 1998, TICKET IN HAND, I FOUND TRACK 5 IN TERMINI STATION in Rome, and an empty compartment on the train heading north to Bologna. It had been a long day, flying from Chicago to Barcelona, Spain, and then to Rome. Coming from the south, through green foothills, the train echoed in a long tunnel, which opened onto red tile roofs flashing between the cement walls of factories and storage yards and side rails and industrial clutter. Through the back door of the city, the train coasted into the Bologna station with its tile and high mosaic ceilings, its huge steel-and-glass front doors which led us out into the warm spring evening, the smell of diesel, and traffic noise. I hailed a cab and soon stood before the Hotel Re Enzo, close to the downtown sports arena.

I was hungry and needed to get my bearings. The concierge suggested the Ristorante Posta. At 7:45 I was too early, of course, but they unlocked the door and with great hospitality helped me through the menu to artichoke soup and salad and pasta and gelato with strawberries. The red house wine tasted wonderful, or maybe I was simply savoring my return here at last. I held up my glass, remembering back all those years, sitting in the wine cellar beneath some Italian town's makeshift gym, my locker open next to hundred-gallon wooden barrels as I suited up in the humid air of grape sugar and fermentation and tannin.

Thirty years ago, my escorts left me in a flat two flights up. In 1998, I searched the streets of Bologna for that flat where I had lived for four weeks. Everything felt the same. Each heavy wooden door looked familiar. The same porticos opened everywhere; there were *farmacias* and bookstores and the university, which was nine hundred years old. I remember walking all morning and returning to our flat before lunch to sit at the table with two other players from Candy. The Coca-Cola in quart bottles was for me, though Giuseppe and Michele thought it a fine addition to wine and mineral water. There was thin beefsteak and green salad, and pasta they taught me to spin with my fork in a big spoon. Signore and Signora cooked for us and washed our clothes. She starched and ironed my jeans. Each afternoon, the coaches taught me European basketball rules: how the officials never touched the ball, how you could run up the court out of bounds before you threw the ball in, how I was supposed to maneuver around a key that widened to eighteen feet at the baseline. More violent than the American game, European basketball never stopped moving, its language a blur. *A sinistra* meant left and *destro* right; *blocco* was a pick and *cambiare* meant switch. My first Italian lessons.

I was a *giocatore,* my sport *pallacanestro,* and because I played center, I was supposed to be the "beef," the acreage, one of the mythically huge Americans of whom Candy, like all Division One European teams, was allowed one. Although skinny, I was confident. Give me time, I said. I'll get the power back. Having never lost my shooting touch, I dazzled them with fadeaway jump shots, but they were surprised I couldn't leap straight up and stuff the ball back over my head. They wanted to see me tear the rim down; that was what they were paying for.

Italian ambitions were high. This was an Olympic year, and the three best players from Candy—Cosmelli, Lombardi, and Pellanera, players I would never get to see—were playing for the Italian team in Mexico City. After practice in the palazzo in Bologna, the rest of the Candy team and I stood outside and waited for rides. Giorgio, the big, young backup center, announced that "We will win the Olympics this year. We have the best Italian team ever."

"Maybe," I said. That previous spring I had tried out for the Olympics and knew, first hand, the physical strength of a few of the players selected for the U.S. team—Ken Spain and Spenser Haywood, for example. But I also understood a traditional advantage American players had.

"Look at the schoolyard," I said, and pointed across the street, the traffic backing up, a compression of Fiats. "What are they playing?" In U.S. schoolyards, coast to coast, kids were shooting baskets, playing "horse" or three-on-three, the net gone to rot or thieves.

"Football," my Candy teammates replied. Although European basketball players would eventually catch up with the Americans in skill, in 1968 the collective Italian athletic nervous system, the habits learned in their muscles, the reflexes were all conditioned by thinking with their feet.

Basketball is a game of the hands, stationary in its historical beginnings when the emphasis was on catching and passing and shooting. Although the game moves much faster now, a sprint and ballet at the same time, there is still no running with the ball without dribbling—a skill of the fingers, not the palms. Good players can see with their fingertips, feel the rotation of the ball when it comes up to pause, push it right or left, and know where the return is. Catching becomes second nature. Blindside a good player with a chest pass, he'll catch the ball without looking. It's a game of brute force and delicate movements. "Good hands, good touch" are real assets to someone seven feet tall and three hundred pounds.

I had good hands, but Candy was worried about my potential for brute force. The mono had sapped my strength; I knew that. My legs felt dead, and I wanted to sleep all day. My Italian managers thought that if I visited Signora Uncinetto twice a week, she might be able to help me gain weight and strength. So Tuesday and Thursday, I walked through the streets of Bologna and found her address and pushed her call button. *Prego,* the intercom said, and I announced myself, and the door's latch buzzed open.

Centuries of need had ground a path up the marble steps. Her door was open on the air of oil and herbs, carpets beaten, a piano in the corner, a candle lit, the scent of allspice or myrrh. The couch for her ministrations lay beneath the window, covered with an oriental tapestry. I unbuckled my belt and lay facedown, my right buttock exposed one time, my left another. It was a compromised position, certainly—pants down, the window open—but I was willing to try anything.

With forceps, Signora plucked her syringe from a white enamel tray, shook off the alcohol, inserted the needle into a carafe of something red—an emulsion of olive oil and wine vinegar, no doubt—and motioning me to look away, she slapped my cheek and drove the elixir home. They say dull needles part the tissue rather than cut it. There's less bleeding. I never bled a drop.

° ° °

HOMESICK, I TRIED TO SETTLE INTO MY NEW ROOM, TO FIND A comfortable position on the wire springs and thin mattress. At night the flat grew quiet and I would walk outside, the coffee shops and restaurants open late, kids sitting on their motorbikes in the Piazza Maggiore by the statue of Neptune, smoking. In October, it was still warm in Bologna at night. Back at my desk, I would study Italian or write letters home. To pay a twenty-dollar debt, I sent my brother two 10,000-lira notes without calculations. Let him figure it out. I filled up postcards, writing in all directions and licking a gallery of stamps. "We eat four courses four times a day," I wrote. "Italian is lovely. I can buy gum, answer the telephone, find my way around and back again. The basketball here is rough. They don't let me play much. Please write." At my worst moments, I borrowed my teammate's portable record player until I wore out my only forty-five, the Rolling Stones' "Jumpin' Jack Flash."

Each evening a few of the players would stay up to watch TV, and I watched too, though I didn't understand much Italian yet: the game shows, the ads, the football matches with everyone talking like a fast break. I do remember one evening a television program that focused on the riots in Chicago during the 1968 Democratic Convention. Everyone in the room winced as the police swung their batons. Not unfamiliar with riot police or hostile crowds, my Italian teammates simply asked me for an explanation. I talked about the marches and protests in Washington against the war in Vietnam and speculated that the convention in Chicago was a very public opportunity for more protests against the war. Our little black-and-white TV in Bologna showed bleeding heads, young women crying, and a helmeted policeman dragging a protester by his ankles. "It's stupid," someone said into the flickering.

"The riots? The police?" I asked, looking over my shoulder at the faces held in relief by the screen.

"No, the war," Giuseppe said. In his late twenties, he supervised the assembly of washing machines when he wasn't playing second-string guard. "The war in Vietnam is stupid. Doesn't the U.S. understand history? Don't you know anything about the French?" I didn't. In 1968 I knew even less about French military history than I did about European bathroom fixtures. In Bologna, watching the news on television, I found the brutality of the war sharpened by distance, and even more of an occasion for criticism and shame.

Sometimes I read late, the flat quiet, the only sound the motorbikes buzzing their way down the narrow street outside my window. Sometimes the walls of my bedroom shook as if a Roman legion were sweeping through town—a rumble approaching, then a crescendo, the water in my glass crawling up the sides. By the time I pulled the curtain back to look, however, only the taillights of a silver Lamborghini flashed red before disappearing around a corner.

Mornings, I would put on my pressed jeans and greet the Signore and Signora, who fed me eggs and toast and strong coffee with cream. Afterwards I would walk again, a city map in hand and phrases written down on a scrap of paper, down the stairs and toward a new direction in the porticoed streets of Bologna. Basketball practice was at two in the afternoon. So I could spend the morning working on my six basic questions in Italian—how much is *gomma,* and where is the university, and what is the name of this street? The little old lady in the *farmacia* was kind and answered so many questions for so little purchase. In fact, when she simply answered without a blink or sounded out the price when I requested some article, I suddenly felt very accomplished, as if this brand-new Italian was now mine and actually worked. My *grazie* and *prego* and *dove* felt like good new shoes broken in at last. Slowly, I would count the price out in lire, wonderfully colored bills in huge denominations, speaking the numbers *uno, due,* and so on deliberately, and she would count back into my hand a pile of coins. If she suspected why I turned each coin, paying such close attention, ear cocked, and enunciating so slowly and often, she didn't let on, and for this, Signora, I am still grateful. *Grazie. Mille grazie.*

Those mornings by myself, I found the basilicas, the coffee shops, little restaurants with handwritten menus, the two towers, the universities, and a good bookstore where I discovered English Penguin editions of Hemingway and Hardy and the Romantic poets. I bought those books, as well as a paperbound edition of the *Inferno,* and when I got home I stared at the mysterious Italian in handset monotype on good ragged-edged paper.

° ° °

I MAY HAVE WALKED BY THE CESARINA RESTAURANT THIRTY YEARS ago, but I don't remember it. Reading the guides now, searching for a good restaurant, lost by the two towers, I debated this way or that, took an alley shortcut, and there on Via Santo Stefano, a small neon sign glowing against the stucco delivered me to "Cesarina." This early in the evening, once again, I was the only patron. No matter. Many weeks before, Jim Harris had said that I should try Bologna's manicotti and tortellini. Tonight, the maître d' walked me halfway into the restaurant, dark and polished in its lamplight and wood paneling, and narrow, with tables on both sides. He seated me before a flurry of waiters in black waistcoats and starched white aprons. The manicotti was superb, filled with prosciutto and cheese, the carrots and greens from the hills outside of Bologna. There was a red wine, maybe a Sagiovese di Romagna. I ate bite after superb bite and was still hungry.

By the time I ordered a second helping, a gray-haired gentleman had been seated at the table next to me. I had a front-row seat, in effect, for his distinguished routine. In his dark, pinstriped suit, a silver handkerchief in his pocket to accent his swept-back, silver hair, the gentleman never ordered, as far as I could tell. The wine arrived as if preordained. Two waiters pushed a stainless steel serving cart up to his table and arranged a plate of greens, and then, in this gastronomic rite, ladled onto his holy plate the boiled potatoes and beef hock, whispered the appropriate *bene*s, and backed away, hands folded. Well, such a dinner seemed odd to me, tourist that I was, but all else appeared fine, the plate steaming as the man adjusted his napkin in his lap and unfolded today's edition of *Il Resto del Carlino.*

When I thanked my waiters and rose to leave, the gentleman looked up from his paper and said "*Buona sera,*" and then asked in English where I was from and what brought me to Bologna.

"Iowa City," I said, and then explained that many years ago I had lived for a short time in Bologna and was back to rediscover something about a basketball team I had played for, a team named Candy.

"Yes, I remember Candy. I followed them in the paper," he said, holding up a section of *Il Resto del Carlino.* He asked my name and said he was sorry that he had not heard of me, but that meant nothing. We shook hands, and he said welcome back to Bologna, that it was a fine city, and he wished me luck and a pleasant visit.

On the walk back to my hotel, I wondered if *Il Resto del Carlino* might provide answers to a few of my questions about Candy. The guidebook explained that *Il Resto del Carlino,* Bologna's daily newspaper, was so named because years ago a Bolognese gentleman's first order of business each day was to buy a cigar and coffee, paying with a *carlino,* a coin named after Charles the Fifth. With the change, the "*resto,*" he would buy that day's edition of the newspaper. Sitting outside in the warm morning before his sweet roll and sugared coffee, before the trades or the negotiations, such a gentleman may have read about the Socialists winning the city election in 1914, or the rise of Fascism between the wars, or the tragedy of the partisans during the Nazi occupation, or the celebration of the first Italian republic in 1946, or the sixties' renewed interest in historical architecture and international sports.

Sports was what I was after. There had to be an archive somewhere. The concierge at my hotel suggested the municipal library, and the next morning his directions took me down Via Ugo Bassi, the two towers tilting in the distance, right through the Piazza del Netuno, then diagonally across the huge Piazza Maggiore, the Basilica of San Petronio rising up on the far side of the piazza—the marble façade never finished, so the front of the church looks formal up to a point and then unadorned to the top, the red-brown brick reminiscent of plain folk, a country church. It is said that after his death, the skull of the church's namesake, Saint Petronio, was severed from his body—with papal permission—and rests now in a silver reliquary in the second chapel of the basilica. His body still lies in the Church of Santo Stefano, across town to the east.

This unfinished façade and the division of head and heart spoke to my very brief history here. I had wanted so much to spend a long time in Bologna, its narrow streets and porticoes and markets a whole history, museums and churches full of relics and art, and the Italian language which made quick sense to me and seemed as rich in its vowels as the good food of Bologna. I gained vocabulary and weight—the result of Madame Uncinetto's elixirs, I was sure. I had the basketball season to look forward to, and nine hundred years of culture to catch up on. My Candy teammates remarked how quickly I picked up the language; the more words I learned, the better friends I made.

Unfortunately, my time with Candy came to a quick end. What surprises me still is how much I remember about Italy and how little about playing basketball there. At twenty-one, I was ready to learn another culture, and angry and confused when that opportunity was taken away.

Many years later, I still wanted an explanation. Map in hand, I walked by the front of the basilica, where workmen fussed with an outdoor stage and a huge wooden cross they were building for the Easter pageant the next weekend. Around the corner and down the narrow street, three doors more and beneath the long portico, there was the Archiginnasio, the palace home of the University of Bologna for 240 years, from 1563 to 1803, and since 1863 the residence of the municipal library. The walls and ceilings leading up to the glass doors of the library displayed blazons and plaques and paintings. I have since discovered that most of these blazons were drawn and painted by students in the long history of the university, each shield displaying an appropriate icon, cartouches with mottos, and the names of students and hometowns. Walking past centuries of armor and shields with pigs and rearing horses, jesters, dragons, and crossed swords, I imagined my own blazon—two washing machines and a basketball centered on a green key, with "switch left" in Latin script above my hometown of Tacoma.

The lady in half-glasses in the glass booth wanted to see my ID. She spoke no English, shrugging her shoulders when I asked where the archives might be. I wrote *Il Resto del Carlino* and 1968 on a piece of paper, and she pushed a form across the counter—my name, *per favore,* my hotel—and pointed through the pass gate and down the hall. I was lucky then, for I found Lara, one of the librarians who spoke a little English. She said yes, I could look at microfilm, and no, she hadn't heard of Candy, maybe because those games were played before she was born.

Young, dark-haired, and shy, Lara—my Beatrice—led me back into history rather than to heaven. I wrote the dates October and November 1968; in two minutes, she found the boxed microfilm, and I followed her through chambers and down hallways, our footsteps loud before paneled walls and puzzled scholars, and then through a small door into a large room that felt august, reverent, and permanent. Running my hand over some of the books on the shelves, I could feel how the bindings were sewn over cords. The leather on the spines looked supple, with the titles gold stamped by hand, the letters misaligned ever so slightly in that wonderful human contribution to the perfect concept of grace.

Fascinated by this room, as if it were Italy compressed, I could have spent my time exploring the books, but I knew I was here somewhere in another life, albeit on film. Lara showed me how to work the microfilm machine and left me to spool down through September, October, and November of 1968. Car wreck after car wreck, ambassadors and politics, page after page of historical sins and sinners, until I would find each day's section of "Gli Avvenimenti Sportivi," with its auto racers and bike racers and football heroes. And there on page 10 of the September 29, 1968, issue was the article "LA CANDY PUNTA all'alta classifica." In my rough translation, my dictionary open, I found the name of the team president, Gianluigi Porelli, who was giving a press conference to say how ambitious they were for their team, and here was the line-up: "Buzzavo, Cosmelli, Giorgio Giomo, Lombardi, Marisi, Mora, Pellanera, Zuccheri and McKean."

My name was in Italy, but I wasn't yet. Candy was still optimistic. "He will arrive in a few days," Signore Porelli said. "The American McKean should be very good, above all, at rebounding."

Maybe the pun was intended. From mono? At that moment in 1968, I was packing and saying goodbye to my parents and my aunt and uncle, who had driven up from Portland, Oregon, for a visit. My uncle, a longtime coach and teacher at Benson High School, said, "You're not going to play for Jim McGregor, are you?"

"Who's that?" I asked.

"Someone I knew in Portland. Best not get hooked up with him." My uncle chuckled as if he knew something I didn't.

"No, no. I'm playing for Candy, an Italian team in Bologna," I said, maybe too defensively.

On October 2, 1968, perhaps a Bolognese merchant sits at a small table just off the Piazza del Maggiore, smokes his cigar, and turns to the sports page in *Il Resto del Carlino* to discover that "Tomorrow in Milan Candy's American guy MCKEAN ARRIVES." The shops have closed for the afternoon. It's a warm day for October. Tapping ash onto the sidewalk, the man reads that "McKean, Candy's American guy, has finally obtained from his doctor in Pullman (District of Columbia) permission to leave." The man has never heard of Pullman, although District of Columbia rings a bell. "The presidents of the Bolognese Society called him," the article states (these were the voices my mother heard on the phone). "McKean will arrive on Thursday just in time to play in Boario Terme. But, it seems that Sip (the coach) doesn't want him to play. He is still in convalescence and out of training, so he will probably stay on the bench, even if the organizers of the tournament want him to play." The article concludes by saying "While Candy doesn't know yet how McKean will play, Eldorado is sure that Schull is a champion."

Doubt loomed already. Reading this, I was elated and irritated at the same time. Who the hell was "Schull"? Lara came back to look over my shoulder, and I asked her if she could help translate. "I'm here," I said tapping on the screen. She seemed pleased that I was pleased. The memory of Candy's coach, however, frustrated me. I never really knew him. I spoke very little Italian, and I don't think he spoke much either, being from Yugoslavia. He wore a sweatsuit to practice, combed his hair straight back, and whispered infrequent instructions. It took me thirty years and a trip back to Italy to find out that his name was "Sip."

From the beginning, he seemed to have made his mind up about me. *Come on,* I would mutter to myself. *Let me get settled. Let me play. Give me some time.* It was understood, I thought, that I would get a fair shot at it. After all, hadn't I led the Washington State Cougars in shooting and rebounding? Every afternoon, Sip held practice at one end of the floor and let me practice at the other end or play one-on-one against Giorgio. In a few preseason practice games, Sip put me in for a few minutes and then took me out. It was tough going, I admit. I was out of shape—out of "training," the paper said. In one game against a local team, however, I scored over twenty points the first half, but that's all Sip wanted to see, and he sat me out the rest of the game.

I tried to explain my predicament to Lara. Perhaps wondering why I mumbled at the screen, she shrugged her shoulders and asked if I had liked Bologna. Had I time to see the museums and the basilicas?

"Yes," I said, "and Italy is still just as lovely. In 1968 I was preoccupied, frustrated." I showed her an October 11 article that was even less optimistic about my career in Italy. The article gave my background and height and weight, and then explained that I wore contact lenses, which annoyed me, and that I had been on the same college team as Ted Werner, a center who was a senior at Washington State University when I was a freshman. Ted had been playing in Italy for three years for Palermo's team, and now the article quoted me as saying that "he was better at rebounding than I but less 'precise' in shooting." *OK. Fair enough,* I said to myself. Ted Werner was a friend of mine, and I knew I could hold my own against him on the court. The Washington State career rebounding record had been his until I was a senior, and then the record was mine.

And then there was more: "In March after the tournaments, McKean was invited to the Olympic tryouts at Albuquerque. Ninety players gathered there, and he was eliminated after a little while.

Around August 25 he had mononucleosis (middle-distance runner Jim Ryan also had the same illness). He recovered two weeks ago, but his physician advised him not to leave immediately for Italy. That's why he was late. Now he feels out of training. He will need, he said, at least three weeks." I don't remember when I might have said this or to whom.

It didn't matter anymore, and it felt useless to argue with the microfilm. Biased toward the "Italian" concept of pivot man, the final paragraph in the article summarized my skills. Here was my public indictment, and as I read, I tried to explain to Lara. "This is Candy's American guy. He looks nice and smart, but of course you can't judge a basketball player by these things."

At that, Lara smiled. I told her I learned quickly—*blocco sinistro, cambiare?* "We'll see," the article stated. "McKean compares himself to Werner. His shooting is OK. He says he's good at 'suspension.'" I must have mentioned a fadeaway jump shot, but Lara didn't know what that was. "But he's not so good at rebounding." No, I hadn't said this. Maybe I had said that I wasn't as good as Werner at rebounding, but on second thought, I don't know why I would have said this either. "Candy needs a big man who rages under the backboard. McKean isn't a big man. We don't think he can survive in the big fights with the 'towers' in the championship."

The Italians wanted "beef" in the pivot. Maybe I wasn't packing away enough pasta, or Signora Unicetto's tonics worked far too slowly, or I turned my head toward museums instead of basketball courts. I was learning how to rage in Italian, especially walking through traffic in the streets of Bologna, but the Candy bosses didn't care about my linguistic skills. They wanted physical strength and intimidating size: this was the Italian concept of a center. The lane in European ball was wider and rougher than in American ball. In fact, it was dangerous to attempt a layup because the standard defense was a foul, preferably the full-body, ball-flying type. Expected to be tough and aggressive, centers were the eighteen-wheel "towers" who could administer the needed fender benders, rear-enders, and head-ons when the game called for serious defense. I may have been "nice and smart" and convinced of my own skill and potential, but obviously I hadn't convinced the Candy bosses that speed and finesse and maneuverability might help their "run at the championship."

My Candy teammates were always kind, almost apologetic. Kindness for the condemned, perhaps. The articles seemed filled with self-fulfilling prophecies. An October 26 sidebar finally announced: "Jim McKean, the American player at 2.06 meters tall, recently hired by Candy, was replaced by another American player, Al Skalecky, 21 years old, 2.02 meters tall. The decision was made after some of McKean's tryouts, which weren't satisfactory. The new purchase is already in Bologna."

Reading this was the first I had heard of Al Skalecky. A few turns later, on October 28, there was a picture of him with Sip, Mr. Non-committal, in his tie and sweater. The caption read, "Last night in the sports arena, with fans and managers, coach Sip tried the man who might be the new foreigner on the Candy team, AL SKALECKY. Candy's managers, in fact, fired McKean, judged 'not suited.'"

"That was sad," Lara said. "Did you stay? Did you see Italy? You're back now."

"Yes, for a while," I said. In 1968 I had been in Bologna maybe two weeks, and during my third week, that infamous second week of October, I was told someone wanted to meet me downtown and that they would provide a translator. All oiled wood and red carpet, the office I was led into came furnished with a pair of grim, official-looking men, and a young woman who pointed out in the carbon copy of my contract that Candy had an escape clause. In her business suit and pinned-back hair, she explained that Candy no longer needed my services and would be happy to offer me a week's vacation anywhere in Italy and then passage home. I'm sure I asked what was wrong, but no one translated an explanation, their lawyers being in the business of carrying out instructions rather than analyzing my basketball skills. I wasn't surprised and had little more to say.

That is until one of the men spoke to the translator quickly, and the name "McGregor" cropped up like a weed among all those blooming Italian vowels. My translator said there was one other course of action. Would I be interested in meeting another coach in Milan to discuss playing for his team? I felt betrayed. The only other time I'd felt like that was when I was eleven and got cut from a Little League baseball team, crying all the way home and blaming it on my crummy mitt. I had nothing to lose now. Tacoma promised only a day job. "I'll talk to him," I said.

In the same Mercedes, my bags repacked, the same two men in Homburgs drove into downtown Milan, parked, and walked me into a fine hotel, the lobby resplendent in gold trim, heavy curtains, and crystal, like an elegant and heavy frame for an old master. What walked into the picture, however, was a ruddy face stuck between a golf sweater and a porkpie hat. I knew him before he even said a word. His eyelashes were albino above watery eyes, and his handshake felt miniature.

"My name is Jim McGregor." He spoke like a clarinet in seventh grade band.

"Yes, I know," I replied. "My uncle told me to watch out for you."

° ° °

HERE I FACED A DECISION: THE GILLETTE ALL-STARS OR HOME. Jim McGregor was the coach. He explained that I would make a good addition to their team. Would I be interested in touring Europe, Greece, and perhaps a country or two in Africa? I wondered then why my uncle had been so cynical and dismissive of McGregor. My uncle never explained, and in that Milan hotel, Jim McGregor spoke warmly of him, how they had worked together at Benson High School in Portland. Wasn't this a nice coincidence? In need of flattery at this point in my life, I said, "Yes, I'd like to play," still assuming that McGregor, like the rest of the coaches in my life—Sip notwithstanding—had their players' best interests in mind. That was a boy's assumption, and I didn't question it, despite my uncle's warning.

Reading these articles in *Il Resto del Carlino* all these years later, however, suggested another scenario. That night, I met the Gillette team over dinner in their hotel. This was an American team, surely, judging by their size, slouching, and empty Coca-Cola bottles. Nervous, like my first day at school, I found a place to sit. Nobody said much beyond handshakes and "What's up?" It helped to know two of the players, Joe Franklin and Jeff Ockle. Joe Franklin, who played at Wisconsin, was a teammate for two weeks when we turned out for the Olympics. Our coach then was Tex Winter, and we played in Indianapolis for a week culminating in the East-West All-Star game, and then in Albuquerque for a week at the Olympic tryouts. Obviously, neither of us had made the Olympic squad. Jeff Ockle played for Utah, which had beaten my team, Washington State, that previous winter in the Far West Classic tournament in Portland.

I don't remember much more about that evening. I do remember McGregor asking Joe Franklin and me to drive two of the cars the next afternoon down the Italian coast to Palermo. Take a couple of days, he said, and the rest of us will take the train down after we're through with a few minor exhibition games. Our Gillette caravan consisted of two Fiat station wagons and McGregor's beat-up green Mustang convertible, which negotiated the Italian cities like a tinker's wagon. Joe and I took the station wagons and headed out, maps in hand. I never thought much about the two of us leaving ahead of the Gillette team.

In the November 6, 1968, edition of *Il Resto del Carlino,* a very short article read, "Candy will meet the American team tonight at the Palasport for a friendly basketball game at 9:30. Al Skalecky, hired by Candy for their run at the championship, will play for the Bolognese team." Well, that night I was on the road headed south.

° ° °

IN RETROSPECT IT ALL MAKES SENSE, ALTHOUGH IT STILL FEELS bad. The new guy, McKean, was shipped out of town. If Candy had doubts about my ability, I am sure Jim McGregor convinced them I was a problem and he had a solution—for a price. Though none of my Gillette teammates spoke of it, as far as I recall, Al Skalecky played for McGregor's team before he became Candy's new "purchase." What McGregor picked up was a handsome finder's fee and a replacement player, me, at no cost. Candy had recruited me and brought me to Italy, not McGregor. I cost him nothing beyond a five-dollar daily stipend, and room and board.

I did pose a problem for McGregor, however. As thin as I was, I still knew how to play basketball. If McGregor had allowed me to play in the Candy "exhibition" game, and I had kept pace with Al Skalecky or, heaven forbid, outplayed him, someone's credibility—McGregor's, or perhaps even Sip's—would have suffered. I could hold my own, as McGregor found out over the next two months. Maybe he suspected that from the beginning. I could have fallen flat, but why take the risk? The best way to save face was to keep Skalecky and me apart.

° ° °

THUS, I LOST MY OPPORTUNITY TO LIVE IN ITALY, AND I'VE SPENT a long time regretting that. The poet Jim Harrison would call such regret "a shadow of your own making that follows you," which can "at any moment give rise to heartache, an obtuse sentimentality, a sharp anger that you are not located where you want to be."

Now, after all these years, I find that the "shadow" has dropped farther and farther behind. Given the testimony in *Il Resto del Carlino,* I understand better the less-than-sentimental business of Italian basketball, especially when the goal is ambition and money. What I needed was this trip to Italy to help me regain my balance, to help Signora Unicetto's elixir reunite, finally, my head and my heart.

When Lara walked me back to the front of the library and showed me where to obtain Xerox copies, I told her I was grateful for her help. When we said goodbye, she insisted again that I see as much as I could of Bologna, and I told her, "Yes, I have always wanted to do that."

° ° °

THREE DAYS IN BOLOGNA, AND NOW ON THE FOURTH I AM TRAVeling again. Candy and McGregor lie in folders, tied up neatly beside me on the seat while the rest of Italy unfolds outside the windows of the train—the snow-covered Dolomites to the north, and the narrow streets and canals of Venice to the east, where I will walk and ride until I find the Scuola Nuova Misericordia with its abandoned second-floor basketball court, surrounded by sixteenth-century frescoes that will always outlast the game.

WALLULA JUNCTION

I HAD FORGOTTEN MY WAY TO THE PRISON. ON A FOGGY SUNDAY morning, I wandered the empty streets of Walla Walla, thinking I could drive back into the early seventies and resolve my self-doubts from that time—me, the big-shot ex-basketball star and rookie teacher. When I finally stopped to ask at a convenience store the whereabouts of the state penitentiary, everyone standing around the cash register knew the route. "West on Rose Street and then right on Thirteenth," they said. "You can't miss it."

In 1970 I was trying to write poems, survive a new teaching job, and play amateur basketball in Pasco, Washington. I knew how to play basketball. But as a teacher, I had everything to learn. I was desperate then to find my way from one life to another. Now in January 1997, back home for a visit, I found Rose Street at last and turned onto Thirteenth—an apt metaphor, I thought, for such recollections. Off to the left, Walla Walla State Penitentiary loomed up again, sullen and medieval. Towers, gates, guard houses—vertical bars on square windows set in flat-roofed, rectangular buildings behind walls, concertina wire, and cyclone fences. As I turned left from Thirteenth onto the prison drive, up again rose the old anxieties.

I played amateur basketball for a team that took shape on the east side of Pasco, Washington—the other side of the bridge at the end of First Avenue, where racism and a tacit segregation persisted for many years. I didn't know this when I moved to Pasco in 1969 to teach and coach at Columbia Basin College; but not long after school had started, a man named Jim Ingram called me on the phone. He had seen me play and wanted to know if I would like to try out for a basketball team called the Dodge Boys. Curious, and looking for a good game, I discovered at our first workout together that most of the players were black, as was Jim, our coach, who asked me afterward to be their center—the tall white kid, the former player for a nearly all-white basketball team at Washington State University. "Yes, I'd like that," I said, even though my ears felt like they stood out. I hoped I could keep up.

It took a theft before I realized what it meant in Pasco to join this team. One morning, I woke to a clanking in the parking lot outside my apartment. It was 4:30, barely light, and I held the curtain back with one finger and saw a stranger, a black man, kneeling next to my car in the row of cars in the parking stalls. Half-dressed, stupefied by sleep, I watched him wrestle with my car, then stand and look toward my window. I dropped the curtain. When I looked again, a Pasco cop leaned against his squad car, arms crossed, talking. The man listened, shaking his head before he walked down a few stalls, got into a car, and drove off. The cop was Clifford Anderson, whom I knew as a student at Columbia Basin. When he took his hat off and started to look under the cars next to mine, I walked outside to ask what was going on.

"This your car?" he asked, pointing at my right front wheel which was still on my car, though the hubcap lay on the ground like a candy dish, holding lug nuts.

"Clifford, why didn't you arrest that guy?" I asked.

"I didn't catch him doing anything," he replied, reaching beneath the car next to mine, "but here's his jack. I can't bust him for losing his jack."

"Who is he?"

"Carl Ocher. Careful. He should be back."

After explaining Carl's reputation in Pasco, Clifford left me to make my own repairs. I sat at my dining room table, drank coffee, and waited, too worked up to go back to bed. Carl Ocher showed up twenty minutes later to search under all the cars. He left just before Clifford drove through the parking lot again. Prudence dictated. I wasn't going out there, even though the sun had risen.

That night, the Dodge Boys had a game at the Pasco High School gym against a Spokane AAU team. During warm-ups, I walked over to the bench and sat next to Jimmy Ingram.

"Do you know Carl Ocher?" I asked.

"Yes," he said. "What would you want with Carl Ocher?"

"I saw him early this morning trying to steal my tires. The cops came but didn't do anything. Would you mind asking him not to steal my tires? Maybe he could steal someone else's. I need my car to get to the games." My request felt absurd as it unfolded, any intention of mine to be comic lost in the empty stands behind us. I didn't expect Jimmy to take me seriously.

But he did. "I'll tell him," he said. Neither the story nor my request surprised him, as if I had earned the right to negotiate in Pasco. At that moment I felt privileged to be included, at least partially, in a community that listened to its own. Justice was a favor I could return by walking back onto the court and playing hard.

For the next eight years, that's what I did. I would teach during the day and play ball on the weeknights and weekends. Our team had a variety of sponsors, including Tri-City Arco and Russ Dean Ford. Sometimes, on the uniforms, the stitching of old names showed beneath the new, a palimpsest of car dealers and gas stations. I don't remember many practices; we just played games, winning sixty straight over one two-year period. All our players had made names for themselves in high school or college—Theartis Wallace at Central College in Ellensburg; the Brown brothers, C.W. and Norris, Richland High School standouts in the fifties; the young Dickie J., a troubled kid but a great basketball player at Pasco High School; Randy Dolvin, the head basketball coach at Kamiakin High School; Don Parsons, a star at Montana, who had started a physical therapy business in the area; and Gordy Guise and Jim Wren—all good ball players.

Even though the Tri-Cities—Richland, Pasco, and Kennewick—had adult basketball leagues, we were overqualified and thus disqualified. Not fair, they said. In fact, I never quite knew what our designation was—AAU, Washington Amateur Basketball team, or random All-Stars? Our pay was meals, motel rooms, transportation, and one another's company. We played whomever Jimmy Ingram found for us to play, including junior colleges in the area, all-star teams, teams sponsored by pizza parlors, cement factories, and machine shops, once the Washington State University freshman team as a preliminary game to the varsity, and finally, on Thursday evenings and an occasional Sunday afternoon, the prisoners at Walla Walla. No game seemed as bewildering and sober as those in the state penitentiary.

Only Jimmy, our manager and coach, paid attention to the road on our trips there. His after-work players, we dozed or talked or listened to music. The first few times, the tension of playing at the Pen kept us anxious on the drive to Walla Walla—and perhaps one other time when we were going to play a reunion game against one of our own players. But for the most part, all those times roll together into the same warm van, Charlie Parker or John Coltrane on a cassette, their strange and transcendent melancholy, and sometimes the sweet smoke. Then we would park in the gravel parking lot next to the wall, gather our bags, and walk beneath the sodium lights into Washington Territory's first maximum-security prison.

Through the front doors, through the waiting room, and up the wide hallway, it was unexceptional, like any business or public building. When we reached a glass booth and barred door at the end of the hall, however, the true character of this building showed itself. Behind the bars we could see another wide hall, barred doors to the left, and a steel door in a wall straight ahead. There were guards in the booth, one of whom pushed a red box through a hole in the glass. For our valuables, he said. He asked us to sign a pass sheet. Then we held out our hands for the stamp that would get us out. "Not washin' this hand in the shower," someone joked. A guard sorted through a ring of brass keys, found the key to open the barred door, and pointed us into the hallway. This was obviously a short version of the signing-in procedure inmates went through to pass from one side of the wall to the other. Or should I say, a signing away? No wallet. No ID. Valuables left outside.

In the hallway we stood, arms out, to be frisked. Hands rummaged through our bags, carefully the first time but more and more casually, it seemed, as the season wore on. Routine. Arms up, someone behind me with his hands going through my pockets. I remember facing the visitor's room and through the bars seeing a boy in jeans and a jean jacket standing in front of what must have been his parents dressed in their Sunday clothes. I couldn't hear them, but the boy, young and blond, smiled in his animated talk as if he had good news. The couple stood with their coats in their arms, the father looking at the floor and the mother at her son in resignation and sorrow. I'm thinking I know this could have been me.

Unlocked now with a brass key, the huge steel door at the end of the hall stood open. I was frightened. I kept my eyes straight ahead even when someone whistled and yelled, "Hey, fish. Hey, sweet thing, what the hell are you looking at?" I have wanted to know for a long time.

Frisked and reassembled, we picked up our bags, stepped through the door, and onto a walkway. To the left and right ran a narrow grassy area, a no man's land, a green moat lining the wall to keep the horde in rather than out. But we weren't all the way in yet. Ten yards ahead loomed a cyclone-fence-enclosed walkway fastened to a two-story brick building. Everything here seemed straight up or enclosed. At our backs, the wall ran to guard towers left and right. Before us the ten-foot-tall steel-barred gate started its slide open. Motors and pulleys turned. We stepped through. A guard in the booth behind the gate flipped a switch. The clicks and whirs stopped and started again, but this time the gate was closing. Behind us the sound was different somehow, a grinding as if the runners, the chains, and their ancient sprockets needed oil. Then the gate seated itself, steel tenon in steel mortise.

Fear makes the dark alive and everything bigger. I tried not to look at anybody as we walked toward the gym—down a walkway, turning right at the corner of the building where a fifty-gallon drum burned and two huge inmates stood with their hands over the flames, a burn barrel like my father's long ago in his backyard. But I didn't want to look sheepish—making eye contact enough to acknowledge another person's space or right of way, perhaps, but not long enough to raise questions. Curiosity seemed risky. So I put on a game face, not false bravado but a businesslike demeanor, as if I knew where I was going—walking deliberately into the building, up the stairs past the TV rooms, the library with its table and bank of law books, and into the gym.

At one end sat bleachers maybe ten rows high. Along the length of the court there was room for benches, and at the other end stood an empty boxing ring. Behind that were toilets and a small dressing room with lockers and a shower. The first time we visited, a guard locked us in to change. We had to knock on the door to get out. How dirty it was, the high ceiling with its paint peeling and the rusty lockers. Colors were burnt or oxidized or denim blue. Crowded and noisy, the place smelled like disinfectant and smoke. A haze dimmed the ceiling lights. After a few visits, however, no one locked us in anymore. We would drift out onto the court to warm up. Inmates milled about. Some worked out by the ring, while others sat in small groups in the bleachers. The din was constant. Everyone was on the move, always someone leaving or arriving or wandering back and forth. High up in one corner of the gym, a speaker squawked occasionally: instructions, or announcements, or a prisoner's number with an order to report somewhere. Who listened? It felt like a bus station, I thought, but nobody carried any bags.

We never lost a basketball game at the penitentiary, although I don't remember any final scores. Each game felt like a continuation of the last and a prelude to the next. Someone asked me once if the prisoners played rough. Yes. Mean. Good endurance. Their team would come from someplace in the building. Two inmates refereed. Two more inmates ran the timer and scoreboard, and we would begin, game after game, Thursday after Thursday, until they all drifted into one long game.

Time was the agent and the tension and the ally and the enemy. To step onto the court is to step inside a timed event. There are nexus points, the half and the end, and time is kept and measured, and only as the game approaches each nexus point does linear time exert pressure. Of course time pressures operate inside the game, ten- and five- and three-second segments during which the players have to do something specific, get across a line or move out of the key or make some sort of progress. But once the rules are learned, such frameworks become instinctual, given, non-negotiable parts of the game, parts of the composition.

What's interesting, though, is how a player's point of view changes during a game. Perception heightens and time slows. Attention focuses not on character but on the event: the pick and roll, the rebound even before it leaves the shooter's hand, the outlet pass to your teammate sprinting in slow motion underneath the ball, his two steps and layup. Or your fadeaway jump shot, up and released. You turn back up the court, knowing you've scored two even before the ball gets there. It's a magic of focus, concentration, and clarity, privileged to the players inbounds on both sides. For these reasons and others, the game is a place of refuge. There is no time to dwell on the past or worry about the future. The game is played inside, at the moment, on the floor.

Each game lasted, I remember, a long time into the evening, the clock not started or the timekeepers generous—a way to spend more time in the gym. We ran up huge scores that nobody recorded. Inside the game, inside those boundaries, however, the rhythm and the movement and the progress of the game mattered: the simple pick and rolls, three passes and a score, a fast break, the back and forth, one end of the court to the other, the reflex and ease of practiced moves. Moment after moment brought into focus: a good way to do time.

Once in a while the world impinged, and we realized where we were. I was shooting a foul shot once, and suddenly a young black inmate in his denim jacket and knit hat ran onto the court and stood next to me on the foul line and mugged for his friends in the bleachers. I backed away, keeping the ball between him and me. Everything stopped. Even the guys who put him up to this must have realized instantly that their dupe, smoke twining up from the cigarette in his hand, was ironically an outsider, a kid with a grin on his face and no clue as to why he was standing there. No one laughed. The spell broken, the court reverted to ordinary space for pedestrians until the referees ran him off, back to his dubious friends who wouldn't look at him.

Another time, a sparrow, with all its attendant ironies, flew down through a broken second-story barred window and swooped between me and the huge bald-headed man I was checking. Stopping and pointing, we both said "bird." Then, at a time-out, this man asked me if I could get him tennis shoes, size 15; his boots slipped too much on the floor and he couldn't get anything to fit in here. "Next time," he said. "Bring them in next time."

"I'll try," I said, but he had drifted back onto the floor. The voice on the loudspeaker squawked for 45677 to report to the warden's office, and the game began again.

All through the games, there were visitors to our bench who sat and talked with Jimmy Ingram and shook hands and asked how their families were doing back in Pasco. I remember how easily Jimmy played the position of emissary—the greetings, the small talk, the notes for home he slipped into his shirt pocket. The only player I ever knew on the prison teams was a young man named Dickie, who had originally played for the Dodge Boys. A star at Pasco High School, he was one of the best players on our team. A six-foot-one guard, he was fast and strong, a good shooter and very quick to the basket. But every once in a while he would come to a game more glazed and hyper than usual. Jimmy would start him until Dickie launched a couple of thirty-five footers that missed by four, and Jimmy would sit him down and say, "Dickie, we're going to rest you until the second half."

"OK, Coach," Dickie would say. "OK."

We all knew he had a problem, but we said nothing. Perhaps we kept silent out of stoicism or deference or a fatalism that wandered the streets of East Pasco. "What can you tell him we haven't already told him?" Jimmy might say. "He's on the bench." But then Dickie was arrested and released, and arrested and released again because he was Pasco's true athletic son. Warned again and again, he had to work hard to get to the state penitentiary at Walla Walla, but he finally made it, possession of heroin the charge once more. When we saw him again, he was the best player on the prison team.

During this game against us, he played like we knew he could, driving the basket strong, or pulling up in one of his beautiful jump shots from twenty feet, straight up and square, and releasing just at the top. We tried hard to stop him because anything less would have been an insult. He scored over thirty points for their team and spent the time-outs sitting on our bench to visit.

After the game, the guards let Dickie walk us out into the public hallway behind the glass front doors. We shook hands and asked how he was getting along, the conversations far more tentative now than during the game, as if the importance of the words themselves made it difficult to know where to look or how to stand when we spoke. He was nearly done with his sentence, he said, and tired of loving his own hand, and we laughed and asked what he was going to do. He told us that a friend of his, who had been his teammate in high school and now played football for the Seahawks, was going to get him a job in Seattle. A friend was giving him a chance. We all knew that his chance lay someplace other than Pasco. Dickie had a position on our team anytime he wanted it. But Pasco was trouble for him—old habits and dubious friends. "Take care, man," someone said, and we made our way out the door for home.

Our ride back from Walla Walla was quiet. There was another

day of work ahead. The game had pushed us hard, so we were comfortable in fatigue and sobered by our visit with Dickie. It was maybe a little past ten when Jimmy parked in front of the café at the crossroads called Wallula Junction. Here the two-lane road divides southeast to Walla Walla, south along the Columbia River to Oregon and Pendleton, and north to the Tri-Cities. A few miles north, the Boise Cascade pulp mill scars half a mile of the riverbank and scents the air at the wind's discretion. It was obvious as we ducked through the door that they were near closing time and that we were outsiders. All conversation stopped. Someone at a table got up, tugged at his baseball hat, and left. Maybe it was his pickup outside. A woman behind the counter backed through swinging doors into the kitchen. The man next to her wiped his hands on his towel and asked us what we needed.

"Cokes," Jimmy Ingram said. "Ten, to go around."

"We just have cups, and the dispenser machine. Is that alright?" the man asked, wiping his hands faster.

"That's fine," Jimmy said, looking around at his team who had spread out in the little café almost by instinct and milled slowly. I sat at the counter. Some looked down at the Pendleton rodeo pictures hung on the walls. It's amazing how three teachers, two accountants, one government worker, a nuclear technician, two mechanics, a physical therapist, and a student can make the proprietors of a small crossroads café so nervous and awkward. But to be fair, they didn't know us. All they saw were tired-looking white and black men late at night, huge men who hung on their chairs or blocked the ceiling lights and grew larger and darker as they stepped closer.

It had felt more comfortable that evening in the prison. The man and woman rushed around to line up cups, but the ice machine was broken and the Coke machine dispensed nothing but foam. Moving faster didn't help. Finally, the man shrugged his shoulders, almost in despair, and Jimmy, who was far more considerate and understanding than I, said, "OK. We'll try somewhere else."

It was late. There was no place else to stop. Nobody said anything for miles. I played the scene over and over in my mind until finally I said, "Can I ask you something, Jimmy?"

He reached over to turn the radio down.

"We just wanted something to drink. What the hell happened back there?"

"Nothing," he said, lifting his hand, palm up, toward the windshield as if to explain to the road in front of him. "Nothing happened. That was the problem."

Basketball is easy. Explaining yourself is hard. I wanted to see behind the tension in a small roadside café, to address my friend and coach's anger and resignation, and even my own. The Wallula stop was not a simple, hermetic event; it marked us as people, awkward and mistaken, who behave well and not so well. Nothing happened there for complex reasons. All the way home, I thought about the café and that foolish boy's running onto the basketball court, how all those games made the time easy and mindless, an escape that stayed inside. I thought about our teammate Dickie walking us out and how that made the prison real, how I wanted to say something to him that made a difference, while my own awkwardness and doubt rose up.

There is no refuge in such attempts. I found the same thing especially true when I asked to read my poems to the inmates' creative-writing club and then to discuss their poems and stories with them, one to one. My friend, the poet Bill Wilkins, had organized and sponsored the Washington State Penitentiary Creative Writers Inc. He invited me, as well as other local poets, to read in a large room in C Building. Chairs were gathered around a podium, and a sheet was strung up in front of the doorless bathroom in the far-right corner so Susan, one of the poets Bill had invited this Saturday, might have some privacy.

At my turn, I stood and began to read a poem about my father taking me fishing off Hat Island when I was a young boy, how I'd caught my first salmon and learned to appreciate the spirit of the outdoors and the consequences of catching fish. From the comfort of my own nostalgia, I could feel my audience drifting away. Some talked. Two played cards. Others got up to get coffee and another doughnut, perhaps the most persuasive reason to attend the early Saturday morning meeting in the first place. Under no clock pressure, I had time to say something that connected, something useful or worthwhile or moving. So I tried another poem about surprising a bear in the Wenatchee National Forest, read it too fast, and finished to courtesy applause here and there, sighs, and stretching.

An increase in anticipatory din preceded the next reader. In her late twenties, Susan had brown hair that touched her shoulders, bared just enough by her dress that I could see a bluebell with leaves tattooed above her right shoulder blade. When she stood up, the attention in the room was palpable. Chairs scooted and shuffled until all these guys faced the same direction. They stayed with her through poem after poem.

How I misread my audience comes back to me now and then, just before I step into a new class or whenever I'm asked to read my poems. What the air felt like inside the prison walls stays like the memory of exhaustion. Those running the workshop—Bill Wilkins and Rick Spurrier, an inmate who called himself the Executive Scribe of the Creative Writers Inc.—tried to lessen the impact. We walked unattended through the small yard called People's Park, where the inmates sat in groups or walked about and smoked. I saw no guards, although I felt something predatory, as if the air weighed too much—

an attic, a dark corner of a basement all your childhood intuition warned you against. I remember how casual and contemporary the place seemed on the surface, the long hair and beards, the hats and the T-shirts and tattoos, the sweat lodge, the lovers hand in hand. Off in the big yard someone revved a Harley, built piece by piece in the prison bike shop. In the meeting room, chairs were set out. There was a table with coffee and doughnuts, and inmates wandered in until the workshop began, all with a casual yet keen air.

Trying to shut out the walls for a moment, I read a young inmate's poem, which was full of strange lights in a darkened cell. When I asked him about his poem, he said, "Well, I was kinda at a party at a friend's house kinda in a bathroom where someone kinda got killed." My silence gave me away. He was from Oregon, maybe twenty, wore denims and a rolled stocking hat, and spoke very quietly, almost timidly. His poem was set in his cell, just after the lights went out when he could think, and then in the bunk springs above him he saw God. The words in the poem were mostly abstract, but what he told me fell to the specific—a party and drugs, and the deadly consequences. Where he stood, however, was very much in doubt. He was kinda there and seemed to wander even further away in his poem.

I couldn't shake the bathroom scene out of my mind. Maybe I should have asked him to be more direct. Maybe not. No help as models, my poems about fishing and the bear seemed too safe, too painless. I told him about the nature of abstract words, but he listened as if I were an authority, deferentially, waiting for the meeting to end. I'm not sure if there was a connection between him and me, between his poem and what I imagined played through his mind each evening after the lights went out. Now I realize his poem needed me to run at it like that kid from the stands, to say a poem is more than just its own safe event, more than an escape. Sometimes poems need the "plain, bare statements" Roethke talks about, but I fumbled my chance to say that. When I mentioned Emily Dickinson's "tell it slant," the young man thanked me and folded his hand-written poem and carried it over to Susan's table to wait for her.

Later that morning, I read a short story by a tall, thin inmate in his late twenties. W. Green was his name. I remember he wore a blue turtleneck beneath his denim shirt and rolled his sleeves up. It was obvious in the tight sentences and crisp images that he had worked on his story. Written in two parts, it first described a little boy's finding beneath his father and mother's bed one afternoon a hypodermic needle, a length of rubber tubing, and a bent spoon charred on the bottom. He gathered these things up and walked to the kitchen where his mother was reading and asked her to explain. She tried, speaking so that the boy was answered and we as readers could understand the difficult complications—how the father had left those things, and why he was absent most of the time, and why the late nights sounded the way they did, and what they must say and not say. There was no resolution here. That came in part 2, when the boy found his father dead on the front steps of his own house.

We talked about both parts of the story, especially how part 1 struck me as sad and heartfelt. But the tragic end in part 2 seemed inevitable, I explained, and when such expectations are fulfilled, there isn't as much surprise or discovery as there might be in the story. Could the first half, developed some, be enough? No. W. Green said no, that the scene in part 2 was real. A fact of this place if I looked around. It was a too-common story here, ending in violence, almost as if the certainty of that end gave odd, ironic comfort. Open endings were dangerous. No surprise was good.

The last inmate I worked with committed suicide a few years later by slashing his wrists and hanging himself with television cord. Between his conviction in 1973 for using a high-powered rifle to kill a motorist on Interstate 405 and his death in 1981, Carl Harp, the Bellevue Sniper, spent more consecutive days (423) in solitary than any other prisoner on record. He threw shit and urine on the guards, suffered beatings and broken bones, accused guards of raping him with nightsticks, and took hostages in a riot that locked the prison down for three days. Married in the prison a few months before his suicide, he left his bride only letters that told of plots by guards to have him killed.

But talking to him for half an hour one Saturday afternoon was like talking to a shy, eccentric cousin, who felt nostalgic about loss and old memories. In his poem "Send Me a Letter My Love," he says,

> *You get a letter from a lady,*
> *even if she ain't,*
> *and whatever perfume*
> *or smell of her exists in the envelope*
> *fills your whole cell*
> *and releases a flood of feeling,*
> *many good, some sad,*
> *often memories, all right then nice.*

When he first read through his poem in his quiet voice, the words felt common, almost sweet. But when I read the poem later, something sounded off-key. Maybe I didn't want to acknowledge the second line in the poem. The last four lines of the poem, however, were hard to avoid:

> *Those feelings are addictive I guess*
> *cause I see guys all the time*
> *sniffing all the business envelopes they get,*
> *smiling when they get a good one.*

"Business" feels cold, a word known only to those in the know, those on the inside. Far from "nice," the final "smiling" in this poem turns predatory.

Although soft-spoken, Carl Harp was anxious to share his work. He showed me a few of his pen-and-ink drawings, self-portraits with leonine heads surrounded by stick-figure guards. Buildings were fed by galvanized and riveted pipes rising out of fissures in the background. Random numbers marked all the walls. Every once in a while, a monster's head, complete with antennae, peeked out from behind a wall. Behind a tower, two hybrid flowers grew, a cross between sunflowers and wild roses, with each petal pierced by a black dot in its center. In each picture a miniature sun twinkled like a star, and birds, not much larger, flew either toward you or away.

I didn't know what they meant and told him that. I looked at each piece and named what I saw, but I had no clever response to his art and craft. Maybe our fumbling for words was a stay for the moment, but I felt no one could listen to Carl Harp enough.

We all like to be listened to, but active listening, even under casual circumstances, can be exhausting. Those Thursday-night basketball games easily resolved themselves, the narrative built into the game. Somebody won, somebody lost. End of story. But after I left the Saturday writing workshop, I felt very tired and more in doubt than when I arrived, wondering if I'd helped anybody account for anything, or whether they had seen through me. Was I a teacher or a voyeur? I had tried hard to listen, to focus on the words, despite my imagining a bloodstained bathroom or Carl Harp on a bank above the freeway, aiming at traffic a hundred yards below—the sights, the easy pull of the trigger, the kick in his shoulder, the murderous insult of ignorant cars. Once home, I stared at the floor. I had no way to keep score, to resolve these stories neatly, as desirous and reassuring as that might have been.

The next time I had an opportunity to read in Walla Walla, I thought about a film I had seen of B. B. King playing blues in the Cook County Jail. I thought about all my trips to the Pen—the kid running onto the basketball floor, the inmate who needed shoes, Dickie's turning back toward the open steel door, the young man haunted by a bathroom murder, Carl Harp's insanity—and I picked different poems. The first started with the question "Misery?" and then followed with the story about being so drunk while I was taking a pee I got my pecker caught in my zipper so tight it took two men pulling, one on each end of the zipper, to yank me free. "Now," I said, "you tell me about misery." All the men laughed and said, "Right on."

Then I read a poem I had written for my neighbor, an old man who lived alone across the street. One day he and I talked outside about lawns and the weather, and then about the Friday Night Fights on TV. So the next Friday, and a few thereafter, we watched the fights together. He would pour us each a single-malt whiskey and talk between the rounds about growing up in Kansas and his own fighting career.

"Had two pro fights, three rounds apiece," he would say, "but I never finished that second one."

"What happened?" I asked every Friday.

"Hit me so hard in the ribs I thought I'd never breathe again. Thought right then, this isn't the game for me."

He sat up when the bantamweights fought—his class, I imagined—and told good stories about the right punch at the right time, how he could see the openings and the patterns, and then the inevitable. He spoke slowly as he recalled his whole body twisting into the punches.

I wrote a poem about him and titled it "An Elegy to an Old Boxer." In his late seventies and no good at being a widower, he died not long after we had watched the matches.

From my window
I watch the roots of a willow
Push your house crooked,
women rummage through boxes,
your sons cart away the TV, its cord
trailing like your useless arms.
Only weeks ago we watched the heavyweights
and between rounds you pummeled the air,
drank whiskey, admonished, "Know your competition!"
You did, Kansas, the '20s
when you measured the town champ
as he danced the same dance over and over:
left foot, right lead, head down,
the move you'd dreamt about for days.
Then right on cue your hay-bale uppercut
compressed his spine. You knew. That was that.
Now your mail piles up, RESIDENT *circled*
"not here." Your lawn goes to seed. Dandelions
burst in the wind. From my window
I see you flat on your back on some canvas,
above you a wrinkled face, its clippy bow tie
bobbing toward ten. There's someone behind you
resting easy against the ropes,
a last-minute substitute on the card you knew
so well, vaguely familiar, taken for granted,
with a sucker punch you don't remember
ever having seen.

Every time I read this poem, I see the room in C Building and the inmates listening. The words connected. I think of the young inmate talking to his parents in the waiting room, and I remember an older man I saw as I walked toward one more basketball game. He sat at a table in the law library next to the TV room and gym, his head in his hands, eyes fixed on the thick law book open in front of him, searching for the sucker punch that got him here—or perhaps, simply, the words that would get him out.

° ° °

YEARS LATER, A NEW GATE AND GUARDHOUSE STOPPED ME A LONG way from the entrance to Walla Walla State Penitentiary. A guard stepped out, leaned down to my window, and asked what I needed.

"I'm looking for the prisoners' store," I said, "and information about the prison."

"That was torched a long time ago," the guard said.

I wasn't prepared for this. "So there's no information in the entrance area?"

"Sorry, bub." He stepped back inside. That was it. The old prison was gone. There was nothing to get back to but my own memory. In the visitors' parking lot, standing in the open door of my rented car, I took pictures of the penitentiary, the road, the gatehouse, the word "PENITENTIARY" in white stones embedded in a green lawn, the walls leading off to their vanishing points like exercises in a drafting class. I wanted to give shape to my memories, to show how fear isolates us all, to recall in words and images those night games and morning discussions behind walls.

After my fifth picture, a guard just off duty pulled his car next to mine. He rolled his window down and asked what I wanted. "You can't do that. Photographs aren't allowed," he said.

"I played ball in there." And then I added "as a visitor," a disclaimer I immediately regretted, the old impulse to keep my distance. "I'm looking for information—you know, what it was like."

"You need Captain Morgan," the guard said, writing down a

number. "He's the resident historian. If you call during business hours, he'll talk to you."

Scholarly and convinced, Captain Morgan told me how the prison reforms in the late sixties and seventies led to terrible problems. More control was necessary. In a section of the 1996 edition of the *Encyclopedia of American Prisons,* he explains that because of these reforms, inmates

> enjoyed a remarkable amount of freedom. For example, at any point in the day or evening, hundreds of inmates, groomed to their own personal taste, were likely to be found outside in the prison's Big Yard, doing pretty much as they pleased. Motorcycles built and ridden by the members of the prison Biker's Club roared around the prison's main recreation area. . . . Hundreds of volunteers from local colleges and the community more generally had free access to and liberal contact with the prison inmates in the Social Therapy Program.

There we were, locked up in fussy prose, the team and the writers with "free access and liberal contact." How sad to think of the irony of describing inmates as "groomed to their own personal taste." How odd to find "remarkable" used to describe "freedom."

Riots, hostage taking, and the murder of prison officers, Captain Morgan explained on the phone, put an end to the "Social Therapy Program."

"Yes, I remember our team being turned away one Thursday evening," I said, "because the inmates had set a cell block on fire."

"I was probably the one who turned you away," he said.

The inmates and their writing have disappeared, I complained to my friend Bill Wilkins, who long ago had stopped sponsoring the workshop. Too much hassle, too many demands, and too many lies, he said. I told him how everything had changed, that an administrative office now occupied the space once used for the boxing ring and basketball court, and that there was no longer a writing workshop or a publication for prisoners' poems or stories. I felt as if part of our history had been erased.

"Remember this?" Bill asked, handing me an eight-by-ten photo, taken with a Brownie camera and blown up until the edges blurred. There we were, all the members of the Washington State Penitentiary Creative Writers Inc. gathered around us, the guest poets. The memory of that time and place comes back—the men who lived there, who played ball and wrote poems and stories behind the bars.

"All the while I was doing the workshop, I thought I was different from those guys, but when I showed them this picture, you know what they said?"

"No."

"Bill, you look just like one of us."

The gym is gone, and so is the spring in my legs. I remember when basketball was a safe way for me to pass the time. On a few Thursday nights and Saturday afternoons long ago, I was thankful to walk out the prison doors and drive home. But how I felt inside, the doubts and fears, won't go away. I keep searching for the words, trying to figure out what happened. It has been twenty-five years, and some of the men are still locked up. Right or wrong, some will never get out. Day after day, we all live with that.

BRONZE, 1936

My hunch paid off. Two-and-a-half hours into an Iowa City showing of Leni Riefenstahl's *Olympia*, I found my aunt swimming beneath the gaze of Adolf Hitler. Berlin, 1936. So far away were these swimmers, I felt as if I were sitting in the last row of the Nazis' aquatic sports complex behind thirty thousand anxious fans. Even in Iowa City, three thousand miles away and half a century later, I wanted to crane my neck, to stand in the dark theater and really catch sight of her, as the voice-over announced the contestants for the women's 100-meter final: Arndt, Germany; Wagner, Holland; Campbell of the Argentine; Mastenbroek of Holland; the world-record holder den Ouden, another Dutch girl; and the Americans Rawls and McKean.

The more I had been thinking and writing about my own experiences as an athlete, the more I wanted to know about my aunt's career. Watching *Olympia* helped to place her in time, although I still felt no closer to her. Growing up, I had heard from my father every four years how my aunt had participated in the Nazi Olympics, and that someone had stolen her bronze medal. But then no one had much more to say. Had someone taken her story as well? I always wanted to ask her where and how that medal was stolen. Maybe the Gestapo, I thought, but I had seen too many movies. "No, don't ask," my mother said. "It's too embarrassing." My aunt never offered.

Our family has always been reticent, to say the least. Aunt Olive is my father's sister. Their mother, my grandmother, Cora Hibbard McKean, kept her own counsel for years, a matriarch of stoicism and silence. After her passing, family rumor claimed she had packed a derringer and sewn dresses for prostitutes in Seattle in the twenties, a Depression-era divorcée who asked my father to leave when he was fifteen. What I remember was a woman difficult to please, who lived silently by herself through cataracts and broken hips in her house full of looms, home-canned vegetables, Christmas cookies, paint-by-number kits, and canaries. More than once, my father and mother lost track of her for weeks, until she finally sent them a postcard from Oaxaca or Guadalajara, the destination of yet another one of her impromptu Greyhound bus trips to Mexico.

In all my years of basketball, my grandmother never saw me play, or if she did, never mentioned it. I don't remember her ever discussing Aunt Olive's swimming or her marriage to my Uncle Chuck, the University of Washington football star. When I asked my grandmother once about my grandfather, who had died alone on a walk in Carkeek Park in Seattle the year before I was born, she said, "It's not for you to know."

True to form, no one in my family had seen Leni Riefenstahl's *Olympia.* I have always wondered if Aunt Olive's concept of "athlete" precludes reflection. She never celebrated herself, although she was certainly celebrated. A chronicler of hers and mine, my father kept years of clippings and photos, records from which he might stitch together a family. Self-promotion was anathema, as if my grandmother's admonition that "children should be seen and not heard" applied to all our histories. Still, a good performance on the court or field, or a record time in the pool was an acceptable display of the self.

When I began having some basketball success, my father emphasized how my aunt and uncle were our family's first athletes, and that my playing college ball seemed like a natural progression. I was playing out their legacy. There they sat each Christmas vacation, watching me in the Portland, Oregon, Far West Classic basketball tournament: Aunt Olive and Uncle Chuck, two silent and sympathetic faces in the stands.

Years later, I still had questions about that legacy. Aunt Olive was eighty-two and Uncle Chuck eighty-four. Worried about their health, I asked to visit. I wanted to talk to both of them. How did it feel to play college football in the thirties? What was it really like for her to compete in Germany, given the propaganda and the protests, the boycotts and Adolf Hitler? What made them such good athletes? Both my aunt and uncle had "early-laurelled" heads, but they volunteered little of their pasts during all those holiday visits of my growing up. The rare times I asked my uncle about his playing football or my aunt about her swimming, they would hesitate, deferring to their own kids, or shake out that old coaching rug of generalities about inspiration and character. Now, I needed to prepare for this visit, so that I might ask better questions.

Here's what I knew already. When I was very young, my aunt and uncle let me play in a back room of their house, where pictures, gym gear, and trophies lay about, tarnished black, dates and names cut into silver plate. Their daughters, Jean and Judy, would torment me, an awkward, shy, younger boy cousin. Aunt Olive cooked, her sleeves rolled up and flour to her elbows. On her left hand, half her index finger was missing. My mother forbade me, year after year, to ask about this too, saying it was lost to an electric mixer. Wearing pedal pushers and white socks and tennis shoes, my aunt lifted to her toes in her own isometrics of cooking, hands together over the drain board, to knead dough for the Parker House rolls each Thanksgiving.

There was always lots of food—sweet potatoes, salmon, ham, vegetables from her garden, and spices she'd grown on the windowsill—but she shared few words. None to explain an inner life, none to explain why my uncle would lean on his horn time and again in the driveway as my aunt misbuttoned her coat, unbuttoned it, wiped the already clean counters, and took her own sweet time.

I know my aunt had little sympathy for weakness or pain. Not too many years ago, my uncle stood in the doorway of my parents' home, bowlegged, his white hair combed straight back. He had just said something to my aunt and then chuckled under his breath as he very carefully maneuvered down the three steps of the front porch, took one more step onto the lawn, and fell down. Aunt Olive turned, a tall women whose face at that moment carried an expression I had seen enough times on my father's face—all animation ceased, her face dropped, mouth closed and lips pursed. As we moved to help him, she held a palm out to us. "He can get up," she said in a flat, instructive voice, as if my uncle were engaged in a drill for growing old, something he needed to practice. He drew his knees up and pushed with his arms and stood, and then walked toward their car for the long drive back to Portland.

Aunt Olive's hair was always short and frosted by the sun or chlorine. She wore no makeup, and her greetings were unadorned and genuine. She had a fine laugh, which lifted one shoulder and pulled her chin in. Both she and Uncle Chuck were always glad to see me when our family visited. Uncle Chuck would haul out his fishing gear and talk about going after the Sandy River's steelhead, but I don't remember our ever catching anything. I do remember thinking my aunt wasn't as pretty as my mother, but I knew she was tougher—an intense, single-minded coach who worked her own daughters back and forth across the pool at the Multnomah Swim Club in Portland until they became Olympic caliber themselves.

Even as a young boy, I knew instinctively that my aunt could drive a young person hard. I never had the courage to ask her advice, swimming as I did at dog-paddle level in a YMCA class that I passed on good, if not comic, behavior. Uncle Chuck coached and taught PE at Benson High School in Portland, where he would open the gym for me on our visits. The echo of a bouncing basketball comes back to memory, as well as the image of my uncle in his sweatsuit watching from the sidelines, and then afterwards in their kitchen at home, my aunt pensive at the window, her plain cotton dress and print apron washed so often the flowers had faded from bloom.

° ° °

BEFORE MY VISIT TO PORTLAND TO SEE THEM, THIS IS WHAT I discovered: In one photograph, Aunt Olive rides with her coach and several other swimmers in the back of a 1935 Ford convertible strewn with flowers. It's a one-car parade in Seattle, sponsored by the Washington Athletic Club to celebrate its champions, winners of the 1935 national indoor and outdoor relays. Spectators in overcoats, Homburgs, and cabby hats line Fifth Street. Partially obscured by the windshield and uniformed driver, Aunt Olive glances toward the camera and smiles beneath her own soft-brimmed hat, a flower pinned to the lapel of her overcoat. In a *New York World-Telegram* photo dated July 9, 1936, she stands waist-deep in the New York Astoria's pool, hand in hand with her teammates: Mary Lou Petty, Doris Buckley, and Betty Lea. Tallest of the four, broad-shouldered and strong from years of workouts, my aunt is twenty-one and participating in the Olympic tryout. The caption reads, "Come on In, It Isn't Deep—And Olympic Gals Can Prove It." In another picture, she is dressed in an Olympic blazer and white skirt and stands against the railing on the USS *Manhattan* as it makes its way to Heidelberg. She looks as if she is having a wonderful time.

To piece together in my own mind what Berlin was like in 1936, books such as Richard Mandell's *The Nazi Olympics*, Judith Holmes's *Olympiad 1936*, and Duff Hart-Davis's *Hitler's Games* helped me imagine the outdoor pool, the monolithic German stadium, the sanitized and swastika-festooned streets of Berlin, the fiercely organized free-exercise formations on opening day, thousands of German youth in white shorts doing pushups on the field outside the stadium, the camera so distant that all the young register in parallel lines, as white and icy as the klieg-light columns at Nuremberg. Ever present in his uniform and moustache stands Adolf Hitler, who first rejected the games and then inflated them into a spectacle of contradictions. Hart-Davis noted that during one of the evening Olympic dinner parties, replete with foreign dignitaries and Nazi elite, Hitler was overheard asking Lady Vansittart, wife of the British diplomat, "You saw all the young men in the stadium today. Do you think I'd let them die in battle?"

An issue of *Pacific Northwest Quarterly* identifies my aunt as a member of the Washington Athletic Club's women's freestyle relay team, which won the national indoor championship in 1932, and the indoor and outdoor relay titles in 1935 and 1936. Placing fourth in the 100-meter Olympic swimming trials in New York in 1936 established her eligibility for the U.S. team, but not for Olympic Committee funding. After the Washington Athletic Club raised the money for her passage to Germany, she joined the team aboard the USS *Manhattan* embarking from New York. *The Complete Book of the Olympics* lists the swimming results: Olive McKean placed sixth in the 100-meter freestyle with the time of 1:08.4. Rie Mastenbroek of Holland won with a time of 1:05.9. The U.S. 4 × 100 relay team of

Katherine Rawls, Bernice Lapp, Mavis Freeman, and Olive McKean won the bronze medal, placing third behind teams from Holland, which took the gold, and Germany.

The brightest artifact for me, however, is Riefenstahl's *Olympia.* After some searching, I found a video copy and watched it again and again to get some feel for the Nazis' grandiose spectacle. Because my aunt and uncle had never seen the movie, I wanted to show it to them, curious how they would respond to part 1, the *Fest der Völker,* its opening of symphonic music, clouds, and mountains, that raw material for the Acropolis, its ruined columns and massive stone as frame for the human body—backlit and beautiful—celebrating, as Richard Mandell states, "the Greek athletic spirit." Did Aunt Olive feel this "spirit"? With much ceremony, the athletes parade, Hitler speaks, pigeons fly, track event after track event unfolds before the hyperattentive and jubilant crowds, all framed by an incredible variety of camera angles, slow-motion shots, and points of view only afterthought and restaging could capture.

Despite the military uniforms and flags, the film's athletes turn and balance as composed and metaphoric as modern dancers. Grace and effort and skill are themes. For a flickering moment, the rhythm of Tilly Fleischer's slow-motion javelin throw, or the grace of Gisela Mauermayer's gold-medal discus throw, arms trailing in a sweeping pirouette, overshadow the swastikas sewn to their jerseys just above the heart.

Each time I watched the video, the years conflated. I watched Riefenstahl celebrate Jesse Owens's Olympic-record victory in the 100-meter dash and the long jump. I had had the good fortune to meet Jesse Owens in 1969, and here he was in 1936, having just finished the hundred, walking toward and then past the camera, smiling and shy, the announcer proclaiming him "the amazing Owens." After he won the broad jump, Riefenstahl chose to dwell on him again. He smiles and fidgets, but this time a hand reaches into the frame to clutch his elbow, as if to hold Jesse Owens still for all time. As the "Star-Spangled Banner" plays in the background, the flags for the winners of the broad jump rise—the United States first, Germany second, and Japan third.

In part 2 of *Olympia,* the *Fest der Schönheit,* the camera pulls back to broaden our point of view from several women twirling batons to thousands exercising in unison. Although Mandell applauds this scene as spectacular, explaining how the camera "immortalizes the [athletes'] actions . . . for the artist in control has shown massed human motion abstracted, epitomized," it remains difficult not to see *Olympia* as an exercise in propaganda. In her memoir, Leni Riefenstahl argues that "During my work I never thought of propaganda for even an instant." For me, the difficulty lies in *Olympia*'s focus on nationalism, the exaggerated displays of order and uniformity, the Nazi salutes, the German battleship in the background behind the two-man boardsailing race, the emphasis on the pentathlon as an "officers'" event for which all contestants wear military uniforms, and the shooting competition that uses human-shaped targets. Would my aunt remember it this way?

Finally, after the full sweep of the Olympics, wide-angle and telescopic, after the "massed human motion abstracted," here, at last, are the swimming events, and to my delight every time, the women's 100-meter freestyle final. The pool fills the camera frame. The women step onto their starting blocks, shaking their legs and arms. Set. The starting gun. In lanes 2 and 3 are the Americans, Rawls and McKean. "There she is," I say. A point in black and white. The film is grainy. My aunt is a light speck one sixteenth of an inch tall. No matter how much I sit up and tilt my glasses and cheer, she grows no larger and swims no faster in the odd minute it takes her to finish sixth once more.

° ° °

MY AUNT'S BRONZE MEDAL HAD NOT BEEN STOLEN AFTER ALL. Darkened by sixty years, the medal filled my palm. "It was my laurel wreath that was stolen," she said. "I varnished it and put it in a hat-box. I had it when I boarded the boat in Germany after the games, but when I disembarked in New York and opened my hatbox, the wreath was gone. Very disappointing. I don't know who could do that."

Cool to the touch, her medal measures three inches in diameter and three sixteenths of an inch thick. When I asked why there was no eye at the edge of the medal for a ribbon, my aunt said the award ceremony consisted of a laurel wreath placed on the winner's head, that the medal was given later with a small typed certificate that reads "Fräulein McKean Inhaberin der Olympischen Bronze-medaille im 4×100-m-Staffel-Schwimmen Berlin 1936." According to her electronic kitchen scale used for my uncle's strict, sugar-free diet, the medal weighs eighty-five grams.

On the kitchen counter next to the scale, I unloaded my back-pack to show her what I had brought—the videotape of *Olympia,* a St. Martin's Press book of photographs taken from *Olympia,* and notes and pictures, resource books, and my camera. I was eager to show the movie to her, but she insisted on feeding my uncle and me first.

"And would you help your uncle to the table, please?"

He couldn't get out of his easy chair. He was angry, maybe for needing his wife's hand—too rough, too hard, he had scolded her that morning, holding his arthritic left wrist in his right hand as if she had injured him. Helping him up, I made sure to hold his right hand and let him pull, and he rose to unsteady legs, saying under his breath how she had been too rough. He had been mean, my cousin Judy once told me, for a long time.

An all-American football player in the thirties, a PE teacher and coach for years, Uncle Chuck treated all of us kids as rookies. Each visit, I dreaded his tests. Pushups, sit-ups, laps around the gym, or an odd assortment of chores—from clearing brush to digging and hauling fill dirt in a wheelbarrow. On hot summer days he would reward our labors. From his part-time summer job at Arden Farms dairy, he culled leftover ice-cream bars and Popsicles and kept them on Arden-supplied dry ice and doled them out to us, his temporary help.

"Watch your tongue!" he'd bark at the last moment. With a wink at the adults, he'd caution us, "You don't want your tongues to freeze to that ice cream, do you?" Set up once more by his timing, and irritated by the misdirection of his words, we'd try to look contrite and hold our Popsicles in front of us until they dripped. It was the same every summer. For my cousins, it must have felt like a lifetime of hazing.

I first heard about my uncle's playing football when I tried out for the sixth-grade flag-football team. I had ambitions to play split end, something with flair and grace, but when the coach read off the names and their positions, I waited a long time to hear my name at second-string offensive right guard. Guard? I moped around the house all weekend until my father asked what the trouble was and I complained bitterly about my fate. "Your uncle was a right guard," my father said, "at the University of Washington, back when they didn't use facemasks. One-seventy-five and an all-American." My father's voice tailed off into admiration. I still didn't want to play right guard. The news about no mask explained why my uncle's nose sat crooked and fine scars laced his eyebrows. But the 175 pounds had to be a mistake.

I thought so for years until my uncle showed me. My aunt poked at his finger to get blood for a glucose test, but he was reluctant to bleed for her. He turned the pages of the photo album with his other hand until he found himself in uniform: 1936. His helmet, stitched leather, resembled half a football turned on end and tied under his chin, a Buck Rogers helmet. In high flaring hip pads, black leather boots, and a black numberless jersey, he scowled in his three-point stance, facing a line of press photographers. The photo didn't prove anything to me. However, the next one did. He posed on campus, dressed in a T-shirt and pleated slacks, casual—an early fall day perhaps, warm and sunny. His dark hair combed straight back, he had to squint slightly, the sun facing him from behind the photographer.

He made you look twice—a square-shouldered, hard-muscled young man who held his own against two brothers and the South Side of Chicago, growing up bare-knuckled and broke. In 1933 the University of Washington in Seattle recruited him to be mean and tough, and then three years later brought in his little brother Rudy, a future Chicago Bear, who turned out to be even bigger, tougher, and meaner. Maybe it wasn't the sun that made my uncle squint. In page after page of photos—newlywed, and then family man with two daughters—he looks straight at the camera with the same squint and same half-cocked smile as if to say, "Come on. One step closer and I'll kick your ass."

My aunt gave up competitive swimming to marry him. In fact, on the birth of her first daughter, a caption beneath their picture in a 1941 *Seattle Post-Intelligencer* reads, "Like Daddy, Like Daughter. Olive McKean Mucha, famous swimmer, and her baby daughter pose for their first picture together. Mrs. Mucha says the baby is going to be a football player." Was this remark in deference to her husband, or a message to her mother? I'm not sure. My aunt's name was Mucha now. My grandmother still thought it unwise for her only daughter to have married a Polish man. During all those holidays growing up in my family, all the silly chores at my uncle's house before the elaborate dinners, the warm carrot-pudding finale steamed in a coffee can, I remember he never called my grandmother anything but "Mrs. McKean." He would hang her coat up and stand back out of her way.

The slip of paper with its dot of blood read 200 on the meter. "Your sugar's OK, Chuck," my aunt said, setting sandwiches before us. In the middle of the table, she set a large hardcover book, the German eagle and a swastika above the five interlocking Olympic rings, and "Olympia 1936" printed in boldface and black ink on the slipcover. Compiled by the Nazis to commemorate the games, this book, titled *Die Olympischen-Spiele 1936,* was presented to the competitors. "Turn to page 74," she said. I found a photo of the three winning women's relay teams side by side, marching to receive their awards. The caption reads, "Die siegreichen Schwimmerinnen der Frauenstaffel von Holland (mitte) USA (rechts) und Deutschland schreiten zur Siegerehrung." I know only enough German to understand that the U.S. team is lined up on the right. Partly hidden from view by one of the Dutch swimmers, the last person in that far-right line, having just stepped up into the infield of the main Olympic stadium, is my aunt. With her short light hair and high cheekbones and a young, wide smile, she looks like my cousin Judy.

What's remarkable about this book is that nearly two hundred of its photos have been developed, trimmed, and glued in by hand—"tipped in," to use a bookbinder's term. Aunt Olive looked up from the awards ceremony in the black-and-white photo to say that she had attended a wonderful party on an island that evening.

"Was this Goebbels's party?" I asked, sharing details I'd read—two thousand guests at Pfauen, a nature preserve near Potsdam; a pontoon bridge linking mainland to island; a line of pages in Renaissance costumes.

"Yes, I think it was, though I don't remember him. There was a castle, and the grounds were beautiful. A very elaborate affair. The food was delicious, and the drinks were fabulous. Fountains of champagne. You know, I didn't drink at the time. One glass of champagne just about did me in. All the girls were invited to the island. They bused us over from the dorm, and young German officers, our escorts, stood at attention when we came in. They were nice looking. Mine had a scar on his face."

Aunt Olive retold her story—young soldiers in dress uniforms, the lawns and music, flowers, white tablecloths, the peacocks, a swoon of champagne, and torchlight glinting off epaulets and swords. She stayed too long, drinking and walking the grounds.

"With whom?" I asked, imagining her young soldier with the dueling scar, the collar of his tunic unbuttoned.

"Oh, I don't remember, but I missed my ride."

My uncle looked up and chuckled.

"It was late, and the Canadians finally took me back to the dorm," she said.

"The books say there were fireworks at the party."

"Yes, I'd forgotten that. It was a warm night, and they were very loud."

Through lunch I listened. Along with the other swimmers at the New York trials, she had worried that their trip to Berlin might be canceled. People distributed anti-German leaflets to the athletes. The protesters picketing in front of the stadium were still vivid in her memory. "We were lucky to get out of New York," she said. "We had heard that Jewish people in Germany were being put into camps. We read about it in the papers before we left. But when we were in Germany, we weren't really aware of what was happening. We felt bad, but we'd worked our whole lives to swim in the Olympics. We were just there to compete."

Richard Mandell says that the "mid-thirties was an epoch when almost all social and intellectual issues were politicized, ideologized, and polarized." As early as 1933, the *New York Times* covered the possibility of an Olympic boycott, its headlines reading "Berlin Faces Loss of Olympic Games," and "Anti-Semite Attitude of Hitler Government May Cause Shift to Rome or Tokyo."

As I talked to my aunt, I realized how young and single-minded she was in 1935. At twenty-one, she was thrilled to be chosen for the Olympic team. Politics and social issues threatened her life's work. She was a swimmer, a competitor, and she wanted her chance. As things turned out, she got that chance. In the end, Avery Brundage, President of the American Olympic Committee, prevailed, saying, remarkably, in 1935 that he "knew of no racial or religious reasons why the United States should consider withdrawal of its athletes from competition in the Olympic Games in Berlin next year." The reluctant Amateur Athletic Union's rejection of an Olympic boycott in 1935 assured the American team of its participation in Germany.

Even sixty years later, Aunt Olive talked on about the crossing on the USS *Manhattan,* the overbearing chaperones, the scandalous drinking incident with the famous American swimmer Eleanor Holm that led to her suspension from the team, the banners and flags on every Berlin building, red and black everywhere, groups of uniformed boys marching in the street on their way to school, the torch runner on opening day, young men exercising before the opening ceremonies, the dark tunnel beneath the main stadium that led to the swimming pool, Hitler being kissed poolside by an American woman, the Nazi rally my aunt had witnessed somewhere in Berlin.

"You knew Eleanor Holm?" I asked, showing Aunt Olive a passage in Hart-Davis's *Hitler's Games,* which states that Eleanor Holm "disliked Avery Brundage as much as he disliked her, and when he assigned her to a third-class cabin, that she had to share with two other young swimmers, she retaliated by going on a drinking spree in the first-class bar."

"That's me," my aunt said.

"Where?"

"I was one of those young swimmers in her cabin."

"Really! Did you hear about this?" I asked, pointing to a passage from the *Nazi Olympics:* "At a sort of farewell party, Eleanor outdid herself and on the way back to her simple quarters which contained two sleeping young girls, lurched into Mrs. Ada T. Sackett, chaperone of the women's swimming team."

"We weren't sleeping. Eleanor stood on a bunk and waved and yelled out the porthole. I think we were just docking. She'd been drinking and seemed happy. I don't know what happened next. The chaperone took us to the infirmary. Oh, that Mrs. Sackett. We all liked Eleanor, but we never saw her very much on the way over. She was always in first class, and the food she brought down to us was wonderful."

"You saw Hitler?"

"At the pool, yes. And one day I walked around the outside walkway of the main stadium, on the second story, and leaned over the railing just above Hitler's private entryway. His car drove up, and he got out and walked in between soldiers lined up shoulder to shoulder. All these other uniforms followed him in. I was surprised how close I got. Someone spit on him that day, you know.

"Then I saw him in Berlin. Jack Medica, one of our swimmers, had access to a car, and we drove through Berlin and parked and walked up a back entryway into this huge building. There were so many people. We arrived after the rally started, but nobody noticed us, young Americans standing at the back. We were up in the air and a long ways away, but I could tell Hitler was speaking. I couldn't understand what he said, but the crowd was frightening—their fanaticism, I mean. We didn't stay very long. All those *sieg heils . . .*" Aunt Olive laughed. "Have you had enough to eat?"

Her laughter fluttered. She picked up my uncle's dishes and wiped the table. At twenty-one, she had been comfortable with cheering crowds, an experienced competitor on tour, a national champion and a local celebrity. Despite the historians' emphasis on my aunt's innocence as that "sleeping young girl," she was charmed as well as pleasantly flabbergasted by Eleanor Holm, and indignant enough to sign, along with 220 of her teammates, a petition that urged Eleanor's reinstatement. But the rally, even the memory of it, frightened her. Not the Berlin streets themselves, she said. But the precision of little boys marching in uniform to school. Not the roaring crowds in the Olympic stadium, but the harrow-straight lines of young men exercising in the surrounding fields. Not the German language she did not understand at the rally, but rather what Robert Frost calls the "ACTION of the voice, [its] sound-posturing, the devotion," its championing of a self inviolate and superior, a single mind so passionate and sure of its abstractions that all other minds in the room salute it in unison. This frightened her.

° ° °

AT MY AUNT AND UNCLE'S HOUSE, THE WEEKENDS WERE ALWAYS given to fishing or watching sports. This weekend was no different. His hands in fingerless gloves for warmth, my uncle flipped between different games with the remote, or slept. If I slipped out and returned with something for him to drink, he would be surprised all over again at my visit or ask what game we were watching. "No, I'm alright," he'd say, and humph as if he knew better, and then chide me for not beating Michigan, a basketball game he saw me play in in Portland thirty years before.

"I did fine. I was only a sophomore," I would argue.

"Well, Michigan got eighty-four points. How many did Washington State get?"

"We had too many fouls."

"Maybe, but they had Cazzie Russell," and Uncle Chuck laughed, as if his remarks had just cleared the uprights to win this competition between us.

"Yes, they did," I conceded, as I had for years.

° ° °

THAT EVENING WE SET UP *OLYMPIA* ON THEIR VCR—MY UNCLE IN his easy chair fumbling with the remote, and my aunt pacing in and out of the room, trying to find a place to settle. When the film began, she immediately set the tone for *Olympia*'s dramatic prologue. "Those Greek ruins look like a graveyard," she said, and then, "I remember Leni Riefenstahl. She was running around down on the field all the time. Very noticeable. Almost the only woman not in track clothes down there. Besides, she was pretty. We all thought she was Hitler's girlfriend.

"Oh, Chuck, here's the opening parade. Watch for me." The scene went by too quickly, though, and my aunt settled in, explaining how the Americans didn't march as well as the Germans, and how the pigeons—two hundred thousand doves by some official reports, symbolic, of course, free and swooping in the film—circled and circled and spattered everybody.

At that moment, *Olympia* seemed less than high art. My aunt was a spectator again, rooting for the events. The film was a catalyst for memory and a brand-new event for her—an old snapshot never seen, a curious document that provided more details for her now than she had witnessed in 1936, chaperoned and single-minded as a twenty-one-year-old woman athlete. "Look how slender Owens was," she said, and then grew quiet as the film progressed.

I was glad I brought the tape. It may be every child's wish to get the attention of his elders. *Olympia* certainly got my aunt's attention. Every once in a while she added commentary—how the national anthems moved her, the strength of her own loyalty a surprise; how she trained in a heavy wool swimsuit but competed in a plain black suit, Italian silk, that felt like you could see through it. Shy and naive, she kept a towel wrapped around her and dropped it at the last moment before she entered the water. How at dinner in the evenings, she and her teammate Mary Lou Petty asked each other, "Did you see him today?"

Each time the camera focused on Adolf Hitler, my aunt said, "There he is," and shook her head as if this black-and-white flickering were still alive.

Throughout the athletic potpourri in *Olympia*'s part 2, Aunt Olive waited, tired because of the film's length, adding a note or two, or drifting little by little toward the nostalgic. "The women didn't have a sauna," she said, for example. Or "Look at the sailing. Remember the dinghy we used to take out on Lake Washington? You tipped over once, didn't you, Chuck, and someone had to come pick you up." Or "Polo looks like a senseless game, really." And finally, as a small gift to me, "My dad, your grandfather, used to love field-hockey games at Woodland Park in Seattle. When I was in third or fourth grade, he took me with him on Sundays."

What a surprise. My grandfather was a sports fan. I know so little about him. Aunt Olive's comment pleased me no end, and I imagined her holding his hand those Sundays and working diligently all those swimming years so that he might watch her, too.

But when the swimming events in *Olympia* began again, she woke from memory. She sat on the edge of a stiff-backed chair close to the TV. The screen's light washed over her face. She was a participant again. There was the U.S. swimming coach, Fred Cady. There were the U.S. women divers, Dorothy Poyton-Hill and the beautiful Marjorie Gestring. There was her friend Jack Medica winning the men's 400-meter freestyle, and then, finally, after all the years and preparation, there she is.

At the gun, "Oh, no. Too high, too high," she says, "I'm behind already." Eighty-two, hair cut short and gray, still trim in her slippers and housecoat, she speaks in the present tense of a twenty-one-year-old and lifts her hands as if to cheer herself on, and then turns back to us at the finish, weary and disappointed, her face half in the light. She looks pensive and maybe even a little irritated. For this one minute and eight seconds, no time has elapsed in her life.

When she asked me to show her that segment of the tape again, she explained her errors on the starting blocks and how she lurched badly in the last twenty-five meters of the race because she had never been so exhausted. "I wish I had worked harder," she said. "I swam the best time of my life."

She blamed herself. But what an exquisite failure, I thought. We replayed the race over and over, and I was struck by how the Olympics seemed less an "abstraction" for her and more a short vivid narrative in one lane with a single turn. An ironic precursor to war, the 1936 Olympics in Berlin was a sweeping epic with a cast of thousands, but for my aunt, the years of practice, patience, and discipline compressed themselves into one minute and eight seconds. The "glory" may not have stayed, but in my aunt's face I saw how one brief moment had survived.

Maybe athletic performance suspends social and political awareness. Although politics and sports have wrestled for decades in the public arena, individual performance takes undivided attention. Maybe analysis and reflection, moral indignation, and social and political awareness, as necessary as they are, would have simply dragged Aunt Olive to the bottom of the pool. When she was swimming, I imagine she didn't give Nazi Germany or Adolf Hitler a second thought. The 100-meter freestyle was her philosophical source, a lens through which she focused sixty-one years of turbulent history.

"You know, Jimmy Carter would have been reelected," she explained to me, "if he hadn't boycotted the 1980 Olympics." I could hear the coach and athlete in her voice and language. *Pick yourself up. Success is individual. If there's a will, there's a way.* I should have understood. I played basketball in college with such singled-minded intensity. Beyond the floor, there were serious issues, real pain and suffering. But I didn't notice much.

° ° °

I WAS SORRY I HAD TO LEAVE THE NEXT AFTERNOON. THAT MORNING, my uncle asked me to help him downstairs to the basement. He rummaged through his bench drawers until he found three salmon lures still in their boxes. "These are for you," he said. "Maybe you'll catch something."

My mother would tell me later that one of these lures, a Lucky Louie, was the same my father had used to win a new DeSoto in a 1941 Seattle salmon derby. The treble hooks on my uncle's lure were sharp, and the instructions still in the box. Although he had fished for years, this lure looked as if it had never been used. After breakfast, my aunt told me that the doctors were certain he had lung cancer. There were ominous shadows on the x-rays. I held his hands to help him back up the stairs, his skin grown soft and translucent. Whether I wanted to or not, I felt as if I could see clear to the hard, historical bone. These were people for whom pain was simply a byproduct of independence and the drive to win.

Before I left, I asked to see my aunt's bronze medal again, and she allowed me to make a rubbing. On the front side, a seated woman—Nike, no doubt—cradles palm leaves in one arm and holds over her head a laurel wreath. In the background, in relief, a portion of the Olympic stadium in Berlin looks Roman in its architecture. In sans serif caps, the words XI OLYMPIA BERLIN 1936 fill the sky. On the other side, a group of young men, each wearing a laurel wreath, carry the victor on their shoulders. In his trailing left hand he holds palm leaves. His raised right hand hails someone in the distance.

It all seems melodramatic. The celebration of victory, cast in bronze. My aunt is now eighty-two years old, and looks and acts like a tall version of my grandmother. Self-contained and difficult to catch, she is still an athlete in spirit—focused, ambitious, critical, and at times driven. She was and still is a competitor—against others, against her own husband, against herself, against time. Perhaps this is my legacy, not of "laurels" but of attitude.

My uncle was just as driven, critical and competitive to the day he died, one week after my visit. When my cousin Judy called with the news, she told me how pleased they were with my visit, but also how perplexed my uncle had been after I left, confused that I might be writing about his wife and not him. "How could that be?" he had asked. Hadn't he told his friends that his nephew was going to visit to write a story about him? I still feel admonished.

For the sixty years of their marriage, each remained stubborn, battling something in themselves and, for better or worse, in each other. I'm sure the competition sustained them. My aunt and uncle's victories, monumental in our eyes, fell short in their own, measured against what could be or what might have been.

Choose not to fail. It's a matter of will and character, they both suggested in word and deed. My aunt, the athlete, keeps on, having returned her husband's ashes to the Sandy River and her bronze medal to its special resting place—a flowered candy dish next to the clock on the mantel.

FADE AWAY

THE JUMP SHOT WAS MY SALVATION. I TELL MY DAUGHTER THIS now that she has grown within range of the hoop. She thumbs through my scrapbook. With practice and someone to push you, your game will get better, I tell her. What I don't say is that no amount of practice now will help me shoot a jump shot anywhere near as well as I once could.

Talk comes easier, which wasn't always the case, but I've practiced some. I tell her that Larry Bird would come to practice hours early to shoot jump shots, and then stay hours afterward to do the same. After John Paxton hit the winning shot in Chicago's 1993 title game against Phoenix—Jordan driving the defense which collapsed, then feeding the ball back to Paxton who squared up, shot a twenty-foot jump shot, game, series, title—someone asked if he thought that shot extraordinary. "No. I've shot it a thousand times," Paxton said. The occasion was extraordinary, the shot routine, a reflex, a grace note in an ordinary scale.

It was those early jump shooters who had something extraordinary to overcome. The old fundamentals, for one thing. Contrary to everyone's advice in 1936, Stanford's Hank Luisetti kept shooting his running "one-hander." In the 1940s, Kenny Sailors, who needed a way to beat his older and taller brother Bud, added a jump to the "one-hander" and a basketball revolution started in Wyoming. You could say the same for Belus Smawley or Davage Minor or Joe Fulks. Whether it was tradition blocking the way, or monstrous opponents—poverty, racism, or self-doubt—that shot, up-tempo, improvised, a committed and solo move, rose out of the clutching horde, defying gravity like sweet notes of good jazz suspended. As the game of basketball developed, true artists made their moves: Elgin Baylor's hang time and shot acrobatics; Jerry West's pure, sweet shot; Oscar Robertson's hard-pounding dribble and easy release.

Willie Campbell was my nemesis. A senior, six foot six, over two hundred pounds, he was the center and top scorer for Seattle's Garfield High School, the 1962 Washington State champion basketball team trying to repeat in 1963. All the Bulldogs had to do to reach the finals was beat my team, Tacoma's Wilson High. Thursday evening, March 14, at nine o'clock at the University of Washington's Hec Edmundson Pavilion. As we waited for the game, ankles taped and anxious, the bass guitar for Garfield's pep band thumped on the walls of our locker room. *Come on, get yours,* it seemed to say. Their uniforms were purple; their mascot was a bulldog. The program said Willie Campbell was nineteen years old and averaged almost fourteen points a game.

I was a boy—a "string bean," to quote the *Tacoma News Tribune* clipping in my scrapbook. In our team photo, my shoulders look like a wire hanger draped with a uniform. I don't remember being that thin. I do remember being scared, a healthy response to growing up in a neighborhood at the north end of Seattle. Ruled by predator-prey matchups, that world found no two houses the same in design or distance from the dirt road. My father bought a house there because it was cheap, the land still wooded and outside the city limits. For young boys, this neighborhood also lay outside the limits of civilized behavior. A sentence in Walla Walla State Penitentiary, especially for car theft, held high status. Given the option to fight or flee, I chose the latter and got good at it, especially during my trombone-playing years. I remember mistaking the glow of two cigarettes in the dark on a shortcut trail in the woods a block behind my house for the eyes of an animal. Late, after band practice, books on my back, lunch box in one hand and trombone case in the other, I had risked this way to save two blocks. Now the eyes lit up fiery red, and a voice behind them said, "Let's get him."

Five years later and a foot taller, I was still running. Despite the Nutrament diet supplement, gallons of milk and milk shakes, four meals a day, pushups and sit-ups, and hours of flexing in front of the mirror, I never gained any weight.

Willie Campbell had muscles and could jump. When the coach put me into the game, my knees shook so badly I feared they were audible. I tried to keep clear of Willie Campbell on offense; I remember the pain when I had to block him out on defense. An elbow driven between my spine and shoulder blade, he pushed through me as if I were a revolving door. He was a roomful of knees and stiff-arms. Up and over he went, and around and through. When I got in his way, my air left in a thud and a wince. I grabbed one offensive rebound I remember. A newspaper photo in my scrapbook shows me scrunched over, hugging the ball in my stomach, elbows out, looking up at our own basket through horn-rimmed glasses, my mouth wide open.

° ° °

DETERMINED TO SURVIVE HIGH SCHOOL, I FOUND TWO BASKETball role models, and my loyalties divided. When I was a sophomore and junior, my best friend's brother, Bob Sprague, played for the University of Puget Sound in Tacoma. They were the "Loggers," and Bob looked like one. Six foot eight, 260 pounds, a half-acre around the key, he would clear-cut his way to the basket time and again, scoring almost twenty points a game and losing as many pounds for each forty minutes of effort. He spent the rest of the evening at home, replacing the weight. His brother Don and I wandered the periphery, listening to records or to Bob review the games from a big living room easy chair beside a table with his popcorn bowl and sodas. He listened to the Stones and James Cotton, told good basketball stories, read Hesse, Kerouac, and Kesey, wrote poetry and columns for the UPS newspaper, and attended the dirt-track motorcycle races on Friday nights in Morton, requisite six-pack on the bleacher seat beside him. He owned the first Honda 250 Scrambler I had ever seen, a two-cylinder hill climber he let me drive once. The acceleration brought tears to my eyes.

And once during the warm-ups of a critical UPS game, he loped over in his Loggers sweats and sat for a moment next to Don and me and said hello, and then standing, grabbed my Converse tennis-shoed foot and shook it in his huge hand as if to say *we're compadres* and wish me luck. A junior in high school, I wanted to be Bob Sprague, eccentric and articulate and full of insights about the history of basketball or Eastern philosophy or Harleys, Nortons, and Ducatis. The problem that evening, however, was that UPS was playing Pacific Lutheran University in the final game of their four-game series.

The Lutes, a crosstown and league rival, had won two out of three games so far, games infamous for their matchup of Hans Albertsson, the PLU center, with Bob Sprague. Each had decked the other with an elbow in successive games that season, so this final game took on a roller-derby grudge-match character. Bad feelings spun all around Tacoma.

I was always a University of Puget Sound and Bob Sprague fan. But I wanted to shoot the basketball like Tom Whalen, PLU's skinny, six-foot-six, high-scoring forward. I don't remember much about that evening's game. The contest between Albertsson and Sprague remained civil, as far as I can recall. But I do remember Whalen's leap, turn, and fade, rising, the ball lifted high to shoot over his right shoulder—his bigger opponent (I think it was Bob Sprague) flat-footed a moment, then too far out of reach, the ball already in a lovely back-spinning forty-five-degree arc before touching the backboard and deflecting through the net. Then and there I knew I had witnessed a moment of grace.

Informed by the geometry of billiards, that jump shot was spontaneous and calculated at the same time, effortless and gorgeous. Of course the crowd's boiling over and the pep band's frantic rendition of "Peter Gunn" have long died away. There have been many basketball cliffhangers since PLU's one-point, come-from-behind victory. What remains especially vivid for me is the game's last shot: Whalen's position, back to the basket, his yellow jersey bright in the lights; the crowd in darkness and haze. The ball passed inside to him, Whalen steps left and freezes his man. Then he pivots right, leaps, fades back, the ball high and soft and settling. So easy and clean. In memory I've suspended him fifteen feet from the basket, having turned in the air to face it. His arms are nearly straight up, left hand beginning to drop, right hand at the wrist bent forward toward the basket in his follow-through—the move, the fade, the reach all designed to defeat what was bigger than him, a choreographed overreaching. A sleight of hand. Intimidation and obstacles and potential naysayers overcome.

Sixteen years old and scrawny, desperate to do anything well, I was awestruck by Tom Whalen's skill, moved less by the fact of what he did, I think now, than by the form of it, the balance and harmony and movement. Now, I would say it was an aesthetic moment in my life. As a sixteen-year-old, I had no way to articulate that moment other than to try and repeat it myself. If I worked and focused, I thought, if I mastered those steps and that form, then all the rest of my life would fall into place. Two points. Another come-from-behind victory, a newspaper headline. The stats indelible for all to see.

° ° °

"TAKE THAT WILSON HIGH SCHOOL TURNAROUND STICK SHOT and stick it back in your drawer," Jud Heathcote said, screeching like a civil-defense warning system, and this was only the second day of practice at Washington State. I was in trouble. My turnaround fadeaway must have threatened his well-being. Tradition dictated that a center face the basket, square up, shoot, and go forward—language that sounds like a frontal assault or a confession. Or a center was supposed to take the ball to the basket, shedding his opposition in a move that culminates in a stuff, or at least a position to rebound. It was the Bob Sprague technique—no-nonsense power and domination.

I could do neither. My collection of models didn't help—Oscar Robertson's back-in dribbling, for example. Bent over, backing in, bulldozing the defense, he would straighten suddenly, turn, jump—hands straight up—and shoot that jump shot in. From the arena's last row, you could see his rear end coming. Nobody could stop it, or the shot that followed. Or Wilt Chamberlain's turnaround bank shot. Not his dipper or his mighty stuff shot. No. I loved that bank shot. All attitude and understatement. When I was fifteen, my father took me to see an exhibition game between the Warriors and the Lakers, held in the Olympia High School gym. The game felt preseason awkward, the rookies hustling to make the team by playing over the basket. Although Elgin Baylor wasn't playing—he might have been nursing his sore knees—I did recognize Al Attles. And there was Chamberlain, trim at three hundred pounds, bending over the bench in front of us to grab a towel and wipe his face before the tip-off. My dad muttered "Oh, my" beneath his breath. Chamberlain had enormous sculpted shoulders, and arms that tapered to thin wrists wrapped with sweat bands. Dropping the towel onto the bench, he scowled and then aimed a stare at my dad, who quickly checked the program, and then at me, I was sure, before he adjusted his headband and strutted back onto the court.

The crowd waited all through the game for "Wilt the Stilt" to jam it through the basket, but he never did. He scored thirty or forty points, one turnaround bank shot after another, choreographed and precise—always, it seemed, from the left side, the backboard and basket over his right shoulder as he turned to shoot. Again and again, each shot impossibly out of reach, as if he simply wanted to avoid the obvious and easy, the inarticulate and clichéd. He left the game untouched, having chosen, I firmly believed, finesse over power.

But that conclusion might have been self-serving. As a six-foot-eight, 170-pound high school junior, I didn't consider power as one of my options, so I practiced being elusive and contrary. After watching Chamberlain's bank shot and Tom Whalen's beautiful fadeaway, I practiced both over and over—step left, head-and-shoulder fake, pivot on your right foot, leap up and back, elbow in, ball up, right hand in back, left under, ten degrees off center and dropping away, follow through at forty-five degrees, aiming just over the front rim, the ball spinning back and hitting the rim, spin and forward velocity canceling each other so that the ball dies and falls through. Or find that spot on the backboard, upper-left corner of the shooting square, where the angle suddenly makes sense, same arc, same back spin—that little skid on the glass—and the ball drops through. Geometry at its best. Over and over. At dusk in the neighbors' backyard, or beneath the grade school basket with no net, or at Wright Park with its chain nets and gang fights, or with rolled-up socks in my bedroom, the clothes basket on the far side of the bed.

° ° °

IN OUR SEMIFINAL GAME AT THE STATE HIGH SCHOOL TOURNAment, we lost to Garfield High School by three points. It was a fast, exhausting game. I tried a version of my fadeaway jump shot on Willie Campbell, only to watch him swat the ball into the bleachers. Another time I turned, and he took the ball away as if I had handed it to him. After my serendipitous offensive rebound, I did manage a put-back shot that clanked on the rim, bounced up and in. But that was it. The rest of the game, I couldn't shake Willie Campbell or move him in any sense of the word. I needed time and strength, and the huge thought of him kept me in the driveway shooting each afternoon all the next summer until the moths circled the streetlights and my mother called me in.

° ° °

ONE THING I CAN SAY ABOUT JUD HEATHCOTE IS THAT HE RECOGnized success. I had used my turnaround, fadeaway jump shot all through my senior year in high school, and now as a freshman at Washington State, I ignored his request to abandon it. What Jud called a "stick" shot was all I had. But when he talked about the jump-shot fundamentals, I listened. How to place the shooting hand up on the ball, almost on top, at first glance an awkward and unnatural place; how the left hand supports, then gets out of the way; how you must square up to the basket and stop the ball during the shot, ideally in front of your forehead, and then shoot it; how all this form means the ball is shot and not thrown, dying as it lands on the rim. Time after time what looks like a slop shot turns out to be two points earned on technique.

Trying to save my fadeaway, I resorted to descriptive geometry from my freshman architecture drafting class. Why wouldn't the same principle of square up and stop work on a fixed plane? If I were falling back and to the left, for example, all I needed to do was imagine a vertical plane through the basket and the ball. If I placed my hand behind and up on the ball and perpendicular to that plane, moved the point of my elbow in there close, fixed the plane and stopped the ball in it even though I was drifting, and shot, making sure my hand followed through in the plane, then, I theorized, the ball might go in.

From the bench, it must have looked awful. Tangled feet, shoe laces tied together, falling back and tilted sideways off balance and headed for the floor, I had control from my elbows up only, the plane fixed, ball set and centered, follow-through, up and arching, Jud pleading, "No, no, not that, oh, please . . ." And "Good shot," as the ball settled through.

When the ball started going through more often than not, Jud stopped suggesting that I stuff my stick shot. At first I thought he recognized its redemptive and liberating value. More likely, it was because I listened to him. Every day during practice we would suffer the "ready, shoot" drill, the emphasis on squaring up and setting, the time between *ready* and *shoot* anywhere from instantaneous to minutes. "Ready," he would say, and I would establish position, hands set and stopped in the plane. Then he would say, "Shoot," and I would jump, shoot, follow through, and wait for his diagnosis and Rx. Body position, hand placement, rhythm, follow-through, wrist and arm position. "Stop your hand after the shot," he would say, and immediately I could see if I was on line and had followed through. "I see, I see," he would say. "Do this. Try again."

This went on and on. A fine, though sometimes overbearing teacher, Jud wheedled, groaned, whined, complained, admonished, and analyzed my jump shot all my freshman year, and then all my sophomore year when I started for the varsity because I was the only center Washington State had. Maybe his was teaching by necessity. I know he wanted the game played right. And by the time my junior year arrived, I had grown up, having listened and learned and shot my shot thousands of times. By then I was as old as Tom Whalen when I first saw his wonderful fadeaways at Pacific Lutheran. My feet worked better. I was less frightened of those eyes in the dark. Though no taller than I was as a senior in high school, I was stronger, heavier, yet more agile. I felt confident. That is, until I heard about Nebraska.

During the fall of 1966, two of our preconference games were against the University of Nebraska at Lincoln. We didn't know much about their team, having no films to watch, but we did see a roster, and there, from Garfield High School in Seattle, at center for the Nebraska Cornhuskers, was Willie Campbell.

Four years had passed. A knot in my back cinched up as we landed in Lincoln, the strange landscape of nothing but horizon and cornfields. The coach for Nebraska was Slippery Joe Cipriano, a name I said over and over just for the sound. Their field house was old and Gothic, made out of iron forged in some Midwestern steel town. Their uniforms were white and fire-alarm red. By myself, evening after evening, I had taken Garfield's Willie Campbell to the basket, or shot over him, or blocked him out. That long-ago high school game I revised continuously beneath a rusty basket on an abandoned playground. But in Lincoln, I felt like a little boy again with a trombone case walking on a dark path. At the far end, Willie Campbell launched himself from the freethrow line, spun twice in the air, and jammed the ball through the hoop in his gravity-defying warm-ups. Now the horn and the huddle. Here was Willie Campbell, bigger and more muscular than ever, pulling off his jacket and walking toward me for the tip-off. At the center circle, I bent over, one hand on my knee, the other pushing nervously at the bridge of my nose even though I hadn't worn glasses for years.

Stomach rolling as I straightened up and we shook hands, I asked, "Do you remember?" Now, I think I understand why he looked confused, as cryptic as such a question must have seemed at center court before a sellout crowd, the pep band rattling the scoreboard with the Nebraska fight song, cheerleaders whacking red and white pom-poms together, the coaches nervous, pacing back and forth and pulling at their ties. Nonplussed and squinting out of the corner of his eye, Willie Campbell said nothing. When he crouched for the center jump, I realized he didn't remember. Was it no glasses? Had I made so little impression four years ago against Garfield High School? Whatever the reason, he didn't know who I was.

At that moment my knees stopped wobbling. This was his mistake. A neighbor of mine for many years, an old man who used to prize-fight, would tell me over the fence to "Know your competition." Willie Campbell didn't know his. And even if he had remembered that tall, skinny, bespectacled kid from Tacoma's Wilson High School, I wasn't the same basketball player I was then. His forgetting me had cleared the floor for me. From then on, I tried everything to keep him confused. Left when he expected right. Around when he thought up. I head-faked, shoulder-faked, stepped through before he came down, leaned one way when I knew I was going the other, backed in like the "Big O," and released for another Wilt-the-Stilt bank shot from the left side. Shot after shot. They kept going in. Nebraska didn't adjust. Willie Campbell kept following me around, which was another mistake, because then he was always a step behind, and a step was all I needed.

The one shot that sticks in my mind unfolded on instinct and practice. Our point guard Lenny Allen passed the ball to Mike Werner, our forward near the sideline, who turned and lifted the ball and caught my eye all at once. We had done this countless times. From across the key, I was already moving toward him. Mike pump-faked the pass once to hold his defender. Willie Campbell turned to face me for a block, but he was late and too ready to believe my jog step right before the quick step left and around, the pass already in the air, for Mike had thrown the ball where I was going to be, and there it was waiting—Willie Campbell just recovering—and I caught it, jumped and turned, fading, the plane lining up, hand behind, and felt as if I could wait and wait at ready, arms up like Tom Whalen, the opposition too slow or late and left behind. I knew the pass would be there, and I knew at the release the ball would go in. Clean and easy. This was salvation. This was the high note in a blues riff. This was Kerouac's jazzy "it." Rhythm and timing and then the release, the follow-through, the silken brush of the net.

° ° °

LISTENING TO MY STORY, MY DAUGHTER SAYS, "I DON'T KNOW. You didn't think like this when you did it, did you? I mean, you couldn't have." Having watched and played the game, she has a point. I tell her it was the best shooting half of basketball I ever played. One way of describing such good shooting is to say the player is "unconscious," which isn't quite right. I had never felt more awake or aware than in that first half in Lincoln, Nebraska—in tune with the moment, thinking and action all of a piece. I made eleven shots out of fifteen tries, as well as six free throws. When I show her the box score my father, her grandfather, cut out of the paper and pasted in a scrapbook, she looks at it as if the statistics are a kind of obituary. "What happened in the second half?" she asks.

The Cornhuskers were a quick study. At halftime it didn't take them long to figure out what I was doing. In the second half, they set up a box-and-one defense, four players in a zone and Willie Campbell assigned specifically to dog me all the way to the drinking fountain. They played in the second half as if I had embarrassed them. The expression on Willie Campell's face looked urgent and a little frightened. Something was said at halftime. Whatever room he gave me in the first half he took back in the second. It felt like basketball in a traffic jam. Stronger than I was, he cut me off, blocked before I took a step, and rode me on big hips right out of the key.

Now he understood. I tried too hard. Maybe I shouldn't have read the halftime stat sheet. "Self-conscious" is probably accurate for what happened to me the second half. I worked twice as hard to score seven points, one fourth of my first-half total. Maybe I was tired. Maybe I realized I had finally risen to Tom Whalen's impeccable fadeaway, and now I wanted to recall the moment. But it was too soon for thinking about it.

We lost the game. I wanted to explain to Willie Campbell what had been at stake, but I didn't know how. "Good game," we said afterward, but nothing more. And I remember the next year being invited to speak to the Ephrata, Washington, Kiwanis Club about my playing for Washington State. When I got up from my seat at the head table and stood behind the podium and adjusted the mike and looked out at the audience pushing away half-eaten chicken and whipped potatoes and scooting their chairs back in expectation, a hundred faces waiting, I realized that all my basketball memories, the games, the moments, the fadeaway jump shots had not come equipped with language to describe them. It was a short speech, full of hand gestures that vaguely resembled a fadeaway in thin air.

Those faces, once anonymous in the stands, were the postman, my neighbor the bookseller, all of my parents' friends, my roommates at Washington State, and three junior high kids who rode their bikes six miles to hear what I had to say. I wanted to tell them about growing up in a family that loves sports, about fishing with my dad and how he was a fan without equal. I wanted to tell them about playing against UCLA and Nebraska and Oregon State. About playing in the States and then Europe, and about all those teams' coaches and characters and players. I wanted to explain the pressure, and my bad choices as well as my good ones.

For years now, through reading books and writing and teaching, I've been working on the means to tell these stories. "No, it would be too slow to think like this during a game," I tell my daughter. "The game's fast. There's no time for analysis or reflection. Even the jump shot is a reaction, second nature, a reflex you teach yourself, just like John Paxton said. The jump shot I told you about, the one that's all salvation and grace, it's made up of words. Every time I talk about it, the ball goes in. The real fadeaway I can't shoot as well anymore."

She doesn't believe me, and I'm thankful. We will spend some time that afternoon at the rec center, running the "ready, shoot" drill for her, and then layups, and then playing a game of "horse" she will win.

"Let me finish my story first," I say, and we wad up blank sheets of paper, the wastebasket on the far side of my office, and lean back in our chairs, hands behind, the plane set, and shoot—the balls arcing up and banking off the face of Anthony Quinn in the framed 1954 *La Strada* poster, and ricocheting every time, *ta dah,* into the bucket.

NOTES

Home Stand owes much to my father, Clayton McKean. He collected statistics, game records, programs, pictures, magazine articles, and clippings from the *Tacoma News Tribune,* the *Seattle Post-Intellingencer,* and the *Spokesman-Review,* and organized them all in scrapbooks. They have helped me chronicle my basketball years, while providing a great deal more.

Recoveries

11 Richard Hugo, *The Triggering Town: Lectures and Essays on Poetry and Creative Writing* (New York: Norton, 1979), 11.

Split Bamboo

20 Ernest Hemingway, "Tuna Fishing in Spain," in *By-Line: Ernest Hemingway: Selected Articles and Dispatches in Four Decades,* ed. William White (New York: Simon and Schuster, 1998), 17.

23 Gary Snyder, "Ancient Forests of the Far West" in *Practice of the Wild* (San Francisco: North Point, 1990), 119.

25 Snyder, "Ancient Forests," 118.

32 Peter Matthiessen, *Wildlife in America* (New York: Penguin Books, 1987), 213.

SEVEN-STEP PROCEDURE

35 Joseph Conrad, "Youth: A Narrative," in *The Collected Stories of Joseph Conrad,* ed. Samuel Hynes (Hopewell, N.J.: The Ecco Press, 1991), 151.

PLAYING FOR JUD

55–56 Jack McCallum, "The Last Harrumph," in *Sports Illustrated* 82, no. 10 (March 13, 1995): 49.

59 Quoted from George Orwell's "Such, Such Were the Joys," in *The Art of the Personal Essay,* ed. Phillip Lopate (New York: Doubleday, 1994), 277.

64–65 McCallum, "The Last Harrumph," 46.

D/ALTERED

70 Thanks to Robert C. Post's *High Performance: The Culture and Technology of Drag Racing, 1950–1990* (Baltimore: The Johns Hopkins University Press, 1994) for names and dates.

73–74 Robert Creeley, "I Knew a Man," in *The Collected Poems of Robert Creeley* (Berkeley: University of California Press, 1982), 132.

LEARNING TO FIGHT

75 Richard Ford, "In the Face," in *The New Yorker* 72, no. 27 (September 16, 1996): 52–53.

82 Wendell Berry, "The Body and the Earth," in *The Unsettling of America: Culture and Agriculture* (Sierra Club Books, San Francisco, 1973), 112.

82 William Blake, "The Marriage of Heaven and Hell," in *The Complete Poems,* ed. Alice Ostriker (London: Penguin, 1977), 184.

84 Joyce Carol Oates, *On Boxing* (New York: Doubleday, 1987), 81.

85 Thanks to Patrick J. Caraher, senior editor for *Washington State Magazine,* published by Washington State University, for information on Ike Deeter.

One on One

96 Terry Moser, *Harsh: The Life, Times, and Philosophy of Hall of Fame Coach Marv Harshman* (Bremerton, Wash.: Mo Books, 1994), 73.

106–7 *Life Magazine* 62, no. 7 (February 17, 1967): 17, 32, 42, 78, 105, 106.

107 The lines from Robert Lowell's *Near the Ocean* are quoted from *Life Magazine* (vol. 62, no. 7, p. 17) and verified in his *Near the Ocean* (New York: Farrar, Straus and Giroux, 1967), 26.

109 Phil Berger, "Is There a Way to Beat Alcindor?" *Sport Magazine* 45, no. 3 (March 1968): 12.

109 John D. McCallum, *College Basketball, U.S.A. since 1982* (New York: Stein and Day, 1980), 7.

Candy

115 Antonio Salvadori, *A Guide to the Principal Buildings of Venice* (Venice: Canal and Stamperia, 1995), 105.

134 Jim Harrison, *Off to the Side: A Memoir* (New York: Atlantic Monthly Press, 2002), 23.

Wallula Junction

155 Keith Farrington and Richard Morgan, "Walla Walla, Washington State Penitentiary," in *Encyclopedia of American Prisons* (New York: Garland Publishing, 1996), 491.

Bronze, 1936

161–62 The photographs addressed are reproduced in Doris H.

Pieroth's "Toast of the Town in the Thirties: Seattle's Washington Athletic Club and Its Champions," in *Pacific Northwest Quarterly* 87, no. 1 (Winter 1995/96): 21, 24, 25.

162 Duff Hart-Davis, *Hitler's Games: The 1936 Olympics* (London: Century Hutchinson, 1986), 210.

162 *Pieroth,* "Toast of the Town," 17, 21, 24.

162–63 The latest edition is David Wallechinsky's *The Complete Book of the Summer Olympics:* Athens 2004 Edition (Wilmington: Sport Media, 2004), 125.

163–64 Richard Mandell, *The Nazi Olympics* (New York: Macmillan, 1971), 262, 266.

164 Leni Riefenstahl, *Leni Riefenstahl: A Memoir* (New York: St. Martin's, 1995), 148.

168 Goebbel's party facts from Mandell, *Nazi Olympics,* 157.

170 Mandell, *Nazi Olympics,* 205.

170 *New York Times* quote taken from Susan D. Bachrach's *The Nazi Olympics* (Boston: The United States Holocaust Memorial Museum, Little, Brown and Co., 2000), 42.

170 Brundage comments from *New York Times* quoted in Bachrach, *Nazi Olympics,* 42.

170 Hart-Davis, *Hitler's Games,* 143–44.

171 Mandell, *Nazi Olympics,* 246.

172 Robert Frost. "The Imagining Ear," in *Robert Frost: Collected Poems, Prose and Plays* (New York: Library of America, 1995), 688.

FADE AWAY

179 Thanks to John Christgau's *The Origin of the Jump Shot: Eight Men Who Shook the World of Basketball* (Lincoln: University of Nebraska Press, 1999) for its insights into jump shooters and the jump shot.

Michigan State University Press is committed to preserving ancient forests and natural resources. We have elected to print this title on Nature's Natural, which is 90% recycled (50% post-consumer waste) and processed chlorine free. As a result of our paper choice, Michigan State University Press has saved the following natural resources*:

16	Trees (40 feet in height)
6,764	Gallons of Water
2,720	Kilowatt-hours of Electricity
746	Pounds of Solid Waste
1,465	Pounds of Air Pollution

Both Michigan State University Press and our printer, Thompson-Shore, Inc., are members of the Green Press Initiative—a nonprofit program dedicated to supporting book publishers, authors, and suppliers in maximizing their use of fiber that is not sourced from ancient or endangered forests. For more information about the Green Press Initiative and the use of recycled paper in book publishing, please visit *www.greenpressinitiative.org.*

*Environmental benefits were calculated based on research provided by Conservatree and Californians Against Waste.